THE STATUS OF THE HUMANITIES

THE STATUS OF THE HUMANITIES

John Arthos

Philosophical Library

New York

Aux yeux adorables

CONTENTS

PREFACE

Whatever arguments are offered for holding the humanities in respect other studies seem much closer to the vital interests of the age. While the need to read and write is acknowledged, and while it is commonly although not always understood that the matter used in leading to the attainment of these skills should be of some consequence, treating important matters worthily, yet not even the most significant material — religious teaching, the history of one's people, literature — is currently matching the appeal of the sciences not merely for their uses in implementing our powers but in providing what it is supposed we need for understanding ourselves and for governing our lives.

Yet it is evident that neither science itself nor all that technology makes available to us can wholly absorb our attention or answer all our questionings. The needs for fellowship and devotion must be met, it appears, through quite other orientations. Refreshment as well requires the employment of the faculties differently than in the pursuit of knowledge. Einstein said Aeschylus satisfied a need of his, but to go on from there to argue that the study of letters is indispensable to everyone, in maturity as in schooling, asks for justifications not easily supplied. Power over language is of course necessary for social life and in supporting reflection but it is not obvious to all that sustained study of the instruments of expression is the necessary means to these ends. In the schools nowadays, after the requirements of literacy are satisfied, all that is recommended with enthusiasm is acquaintance with contemporary works of fiction even though these serve only ephemeral interests, leaving hardly more impression than newspapers. Support of this kind underlines the comment of

1

Giuseppe Toffanin, that "the world has never so often and so lyrically sung the praises of humanistic education as since the discovery that it amounts to nonsense."

In earlier times in Europe and America it was thought wise to feed the child's interest in language with literature, focusing on the works of the Greeks and Romans, and first-hand knowledge of the languages themselves was recommended as the means of consolidating the cultures of people everywhere on the globe. While it remains true that these studies are of incomparable value there are many reasons to refuse them the place they once had. Ananda Coomaraswamy made a point about the imposition of the British form of classical education upon his people that may be extended: it turned educated Indians into "a generation of spiritual bastards and intellectual pariahs." Yet to advocate exclusive or even primary attention to a people's own traditions is to risk too costly a provinciality. And so in recent years we find an organization taking form in Europe to oppose the relativism implicit in such a policy, advancing claims for a program of education designed to inculcate the principles of "the one self-evident civilization." In place of the confusion of Babel education would demonstrate the primacy of the cultures deriving from Indo-European originals, by this means returning to authority in the minds of all "the ethics and aesthetics that have their center in Athens, Rome, Persepolis, and the Celtic forests." (*Le groupement de recherches et d'études de la civilisation europééne —* G. R. E. C. E.) The argument is to this effect: For each people to set supreme value upon its own culture ends in egalitarianism; when no culture may be preferred to any other the way is clear for "the tyranny of industrial materialism and the planetary consumer society." This is barbarism, and to escape this we must return to the idea of aristocracy: education everywhere must uphold the hierarchy of values the ancients made known to the world in cultivating rationality and nobility. The old idea has come forward in a new dress.

It has of course been "social studies" forwarded in the name of scientific objectivity that have largely undermined the position of classicists and almost as effectively limited efforts to give primacy to the transmission of indigenous cultures. As with the physical sciences that provide the models these do not allow for discriminations with respect to worth, and as the analyses of the activities of humans become more refined and more extensive it is less and less possible to obtain from them anything more than descriptions and comparisons of the workings of imprecisely categorized groups. Such studies give as little support to Coomaraswamy's preference of his native culture as to the universalism that in educating Indians turned them into pariahs.

The searching and wide-ranging reasoning of Max Weber is everywhere at work in the modern movement, and especially through the proposition that we must depend upon value-free analysis in discovering the elements of human behavior and groupings. Pursuing this faithfully we may expect to arrive at understanding free from the parochial distortions our own culture imposes upon our thinking, and we shall escape the confusion that follows when we are governed by prior commitments to ideas of "the essentially human," or of "civilization."

The successes of the objective mentality in advancing knowledge in the physical and natural sciences have led to their use as models for the study of human matters, for "human sciences." Organizations of specialists assemble data from the lives of people everywhere in order to substantiate the claim to scientific status — faithfulness to fact and exhaustiveness preparing for such generalizations and theories as observation and experiment may substantiate. The effort is as unremitting in opposing traditional, unscientific ways as that required of scientists in the Renaissance in opposing the Aristoteleans. From the beginning the very concept of "value-free" confronted the universal disposition to suppose inherent worth in every aspect of human concern, but more than that, it met, as it continues to meet, the charge of incoherence, setting a value, and the highest value, upon the idea of value-freedom. The criticism is pursued to the point that the charge finally made is that a consistent effort to maintain the authority of objectivity in the study of human affairs ends in nihilism: ". . . for Weber, in his capacity as a social philosopher, excellence and baseness lost their primary meaning. Excellence now means devotion to a cause, be it good or evil, and baseness means indifference to all causes. Excellence and baseness thus understood are excellence and baseness of a higher order. They belong to a dimension that is exalted far above the dimension of action. They can be seen only after one has completely broken away from the world in which we have to make decisions, although they present themselves as preceding any decision. They are the correlates of a purely theoretical attitude toward the world of action. That theoretical attitude implies equal respect for all causes; but such respect is possible only for him who is not devoted to any cause. Now if excellence is devotion to a cause and baseness indifference to all causes, the theoretical attitude toward all causes would have to be qualified as base. No wonder, then, that Weber was driven to question the value of theory, of science, of reason, of the realm of the mind, and therewith of both the moral imperatives and the cultural values."[1]

The criticism goes still further. Not only has the scientist as nihilist disqualified himself from communicating with those who are not nihilists, he undermines the moralities of peoples and he requires their discrediting — that is to say, he propagates his own doctrines: "To create social science is to influence society in its very method of making fundamental choices, and it is to expect society to manage itself in a scientific way. . . . The discipline and rationality of the social sciences have understandably placed so much stress on calculability and determinism that they contributed to the weakening in man's faith in eschatalogical and nonscientific categories. In this way the influence of social science on society has been doctrinaire and ideological."[2]

The charge of nihilism is not often acknowledged in professional writings but that of mechanicism — on analogy with a common drift in the physical sciences — is affirmed constantly in "systems" approaches that also depend upon value-free procedures. There are some who would even think acceptable Leo Apostel's definition of humans: "Man is a complex error-controlled regulator, restoring its continually disturbed equilibrium through compensatory actions executed by many superimposed feedback cycles, obeying criteria of efficiency, which are not predetermined forever."[3]

Not all social scientists will agree to so precise a formulation, but the failure to prize discrimination in ethics and aesthetics must lead to something like this if the model of the physical sciences is to be retained. What is ultimately at issue is the propriety of regarding human matters in the light of the abstractions all science cultivates at the expense of particulars, the interest in discovering order amongst the disorder of an infinite number of particularities, classifying and generalizing, and, in some circum-

4

stances, quantifying. The issue is pointed to in the objection so often made that a human being is not a number.

There are, of course, many different orientations among social scientists, some more rigidly positivist or determinist than others; there are those who even within a strictly defined materialism allow for a degree of freedom in the actions of humans. There are Marxists who in paying honor to history and historic process assign roles, however limited, for individuals to assume. These often make serious efforts to accommodate certain of the interests and values of those traditionally called humanists to their own historical materialism. Bridges have even been made to religious doctrine. Such efforts, however limited the successes so far, do testify to respect for a definable character in humans to be discovered when holding the "right" historical perspective.

In limiting the province of science value-free analysis makes as little as it can of history; its scope would be complete if the dimension of time could be ignored, yet science itself has a history and it is when we take this into view that we discover the grounds for allying the undertakings of science to the humanities and thereby open the way to a rebuttal of the nihilists. John Burnet, the historian of ancient thought, made the essential point long ago in commenting on the origins of science in Greece: "The true Hellenist will never be hostile to science, for he cannot be so without being faithless to Hellenism, and the true student of science will not be hostile to Hellenism when he sees that his own work was begun at Miletus and Croton. The spirit of science was the same then as now, and the methods of observation and experiment were the same in all essentials, however much they may have been perfected since."[4]

Of course the scientifically oriented objectivist could disallow this partnership, believing that only processes that are presently observable provide allowable matter for study. In general, he could agree with Burnet only if he is prepared to examine the prescription for objectivity as founded in a historic process and therefore subject to such scrutiny as historical perspective insists upon. He would then be faced with the question — Is objective practice itself free from cultural delimiting?

This questioning is indeed called for, and the answers increasingly pointed. And indeed if we should be as careful in referring the developments in scientific procedures to philosophic and social orientations as we are in studying human customs we might hope, with Burnet, to regain a sense of proportion in assessing the uses of objectivity. The conclusions of nihilism would not go uncontested since we might again be able to give weight to satisfactions objectivity knows nothing of.

But then, just as it appears that the re-institution of historical perspective might undermine the claims of objectivity to unconditional authority, we are met with the most unsettling rejoinder of all.

Those who hold to tradition assure us there is nothing new under the sun, and among the constants is the certainty that death sets a limit to life. They resist the predictions now being made in the name of science and technology that not only the race's but the individual's life may be prolonged indefinitely. They observe what is obvious, the general increase in the life-span, but they rebel against all that suggests that life could go on indefinitely.

Hitherto humans have thought of life as measured, have looked forward to growth and maturing and decay, to the crowning of experience with wisdom, and to a timely end. It has been understood that death is the price paid for life, and there has always been in some form — explicitly for the religious — the thought of an accounting. The journey, the pilgrimage, the adventure — whatever — looks to its conclusion; for the hero, dying gloriously; for others, generally as it was with Prospero seeing his child embarked upon a hopeful future, every third thought his grave. And now this — just when we may have believed that the historical perspective had been forced upon those committed to the value-free pursuit of truth, and the inadequacy of timeless objectivity exposed — "thought without a thinker" — the practical successes this procedure has attained bring into question the reasoning of traditionalists at the very center of their understanding, the certainty of death.

And now: "Death no longer appears as a necessity belonging to the nature of life, but as an avoidable, at least in principle tractable and long-delayable, organic malfunction . . . the promised gift raises questions never to be asked before in terms of practical choice, and that no principle of former ethics, which took the human constant for granted, is competent to deal with. . . . It is similar with all the other, quasiutopian powers about to be made

6

available by the advances of biomedical science as they are translated into technology."[5]

The inferences are permeating minds everywhere, not only affecting philosophy and morality but weighing upon consciousness itself. How deeply this has taken hold, and how its significance is understood, is revealed impressively in a recent novel from Africa. A young man has been taken from the rich life of his tribe to study in France. He meets with Descartes and Pascal and with all that followed from them and so he is able to comprehend the full force of the modern transformation: "Down there [in Diallobé] between death and myself there was intimacy, made up both of my terror and my expectation. Here [in Paris] death has become a stranger to me. I forget about it. When I try to think about it I see only a dried-out feeling, an abstract eventuality, scarcely more disagreeable to me than to my insurance company."[6] For him life has become poorer, being reduced to what is mechanically tractable, whereby it is almost devoid of interest, and poorer also because it is to be endless, which is to say, offering only the prospect of interminable, pointless existence. The prospect of infinity so understood seems to deprive life of its savor.

To permeate consciousness is one thing, to overcome the doubt that technology will make good on its promises is another. "Mankind has not yet completed the enormous structure erected by Einstein, Freud and Pavlov, the work has only begun, and the results are still incalculable. Nevertheless, one may doubt that science will in the end carry everything before it, once and for all, that it will succeed in mastering the whole of human experience. Sooner or later one expects that it will run up against a limit. The trouble is that at the moment one cannot say what that limit will be, nor even what will offer hindrances. One thing is certain, mere wishing will not provide them, it must be thought itself that offers opposition, and it is precisely in that realm that we are now disarmed."[7]

And so the thought of the unimpeded success rankles — the prospect of life continuing without discernible limits, attained through the value-free manipulation of techniques, thereafter subject to like interminable manipulation, physically and in "behavior modification," and so leading us to question, even to abandon, what all previously have held to as the measure of the good

7

use of — in the unavoidable phrase — our alloted time. Now, it appears, the machine is to be kept in good running order forever. The implication is clear — running for the sake of running, survival the single objective.

In an early Greek view — shared in many parts of the earth — men were thought of as beings superior to animals although inferior to gods. Like the gods in possessing speech and reason, they were yet weaker, they seldom rivalled them in beauty, and they were mortal. But within these limits they might reach a fullness of being denied to animals. For most, as now, life was nasty, brutish, and short, but there were some so blessed — sometimes through the favor of the gods, sometimes through their own endowments and efforts — who attained such ease and gentleness and strength, poise, and the grace of generosity, they became a beacon to the rest. Bruno Snell saw this flowering first in the society represented in Menander's plays. Many observe the like elsewhere as well, in the evidence of certain Chinese sculptures, in the finest Eastern architecture, in the music of many peoples. Close enough to our own time we perceive this in the gentleness Erasmus pointed to in More, in the comradeship of Ficino and Cavalcanti from the time they were children — "an infectious sweetness of disposition, friendship being their chief pleasure."

All of us learn of this from time to time through experience but we require the testimony of the finest expressions to sustain our valuings of its importance. It is through the records of history and the arts that we receive the invaluable confirmation, the forms that acquaint us with the range of depth and fineness in the grace of those who for some while escaped the world's great snare uncaught.

The subject matter of what was to be called humanistic study was just this gracing of mortal life. What had come about through the fortunate circumstances of Attic life the Romans undertook to emulate through study of the models of expression re-creating this excellence, through the writings of Menander for one, and in time through philosophic and moral teaching, with Cicero the most marvellous proponent. The entire enterprise rested upon the understanding of the nature of dignity and nobility, agreement upon the ends of life, respect for the labor undertaken to attain those ends, all made possible in the confidence that through the free play of judgment thought and passion might be harmonized, principle enthroned.

In the Renaissance Pico della Mirandola as so many others laid out schemes of the entire universe in supporting the idea of a privileged place for humans within it, a dignity deserved through exercising the freedom that enabled them to follow where reason led. These cosmologies have since been abandoned but for some the faith remains in a privileged place for humans who are able to range freely in thought and now in space itself. The famous words of Hamlet are now colored with nostalgia for a lost assurance but they are still far from meaningless —

> What a piece of work is man! How noble in reason, how infinite in faculty, in form and moving how express and admirable! In action how like an angel, in apprehension how like a god! The beauty of the world, the paragon of animals. . . .

Such faith as remains resists the intimidations of behaviorists and determinists, however ironclad the logic — that limiting formalization as Piaget speaks of it[8] — and however provocative the experiments that support the view of human life as functioning or malfunctioning matter. The traditionalist, however much confounded by circumstances never met with before, holds fast to his doubts. When he does not appeal to religious instruction he may appeal to a cardinal affirmation of what is called humanism — "the refusal of our very being to be taken in by anything that presents itself as entirely new."[9]

Such doubt is in effect a refusal that is believed to be grounded in nature. One may remark the obvious — that the processes of death are as intermingled with life as dark with light, but the main consideration is another — that death by definition is the absence of life, and thought itself cannot treat of one apart from the other.

In short, to make an effort nowadays to maintain anything like the respect for the humanities which once was held requires more than an appeal to ancient pieties. The profoundest orientations of modern Western culture are at issue. Many wise critics are engaged in attempts to resolve the crucial disputes, and the present effort to come to terms with the crisis is confessedly a modest one. My possibly allowable ambition is to order some arguments in ways acceptable to common sense to maintain something of

9

value that is being neglected, to insist that the case for the humanities rests upon philosophic foundations, and ultimately metaphysics, and that the confusion that prevails in the schools and in criticism is compounded by the failure to hold to account for their philosophic justification the partisans of those studies that have superseded the study of language and literature.

NOTES

[1] Leo Strauss, *Natural Right and History*, Chicago, 1953, p. 46.

[2] Paul Halmos, quoted by T. S. Simey, *Social Science and Social Purpose*, London, 1968, p. 177.

[3] Quoted by W. J. M. Mackenzie, *Politics and Social Science*, Harmondsworth, 1967, p. 108.

[4] *Essays and Addresses*, London, 1929, p. 125.

[5] Hans Jonas, *Philosophical Essays*, Englewood Cliffs, 1974, p. 15.

[6] C. H. Kane, *Ambiguous Adventure*, translated by Katherine Woods, New York, p. 149.

[7] Gérard Bonnot, *Ils Ont Tué Descartes*, Paris, 1969, p. 251.

[8] ". . . there are many different logics, and not just a single logic. This means that no single logic is strong enough to support the total construction of human knowledge. But it also means that, when all the different logics are taken together, they are not sufficiently coherent with one another to serve as the foundation for human knowledge. Any one logic, then, is too weak, but all the logics, taken together, are too rich to enable logic to form a single value basis for knowledge. That is the first reason why formalization alone is not sufficient." Jean Piaget, *Genetic Epistemology*, translated by Eleanor Duckworth, New York: Columbia University Press, 1970, pp. 10-11.

[9] Fernand Robert, *L'Humanisme*, Paris, 1946, p. 152.

Solomon and the Queen of Sheba

I

In devising programs of study to induct new generations into the society in which technology is changing so many relationships and leading us to expect more change to come, the schools may succeed fairly well in presenting the knowledge and developing skills the cult of power requires. The subjects studied in the pure and applied sciences provide directions for answering the questions they put, but the answers looked for in the study of human activities are not as obviously implicit in the questioning. This is true even when mechanical systems or mathematical relationships are proposed as the ultimate forms of individual and social life. Yet we continue to try to make the study of human affairs into sciences like these others, to reach for similar successes, to discover such regularities in human orderings as will enable prediction and in the end make possible the control of behavior and even consciousness. Once such results were clearly in view patterns for education could be definitely laid down.

Meanwhile there are disappointments and much uncertainty. Now this approach, now that is followed, and once-assured dogmas are steadily overthrown. We explain the failures in a couple of ways. We judge the techniques we employ in our studies and instruction to be inadequate, or else we do not have enough facts, or the right ones, to go on. Whatever the reasons, the failures of economics, sociology, and psychology to lead to descriptions and principles as satisfactory and efficacious as the physical sciences have at their disposal have not discouraged massive efforts to construct models of all organic and psychological and social activities, and to discover the techniques of manipulating states of mind and conduct by methods comparable to those in use in the manipulation of matter. Consequently programs of education change so frequently that we feel justified in believing we have often been taken in by fashion.

So many economic and social relationships have been transformed that much earlier teaching is thought to be pointless. This, of course, is but one phase of more general upheavals. Philosophies disintegrate, secularism replaces religion, ethics become relative, and we are advised to look for guidance in this changing world to our single sure knowledge, the ways of mechanical operations, which include, in Swift's words, "the mechanical operations of the spirit." We are to govern ourselves, in short, in the light of what is technologically possible. Learning to manage ever increasing resources we come to believe that in the past it was ignorance not incapacity that subjected us to vicissitudes we no longer need to suffer. But if old landmarks are of no use, new ones disappear as quickly as we look to them. It is not only that changes are proceeding rapidly, again and again consequences — "side-effects" among others — are unforeseeable. For two or three centuries at least the drift of philosophy and science has been towards the destruction of claims for the validity of absolute truths and universal norms, and now, with the support of the experimental — the explorations of space, investigations into the chemical constituents of life, the soundings of the influence of the unconscious — we look towards an apparently endless reordering of continually changing circumstances.

If we were to try to estimate the character of the new conditions, comparing, say, the concerns of the crowds on the streets of New York now with what was filling the minds of the people of Alexandria in ancient Egypt, we would notice how much more the moderns are absorbed with hopes and plans for changing our environment. The streets themselves are very different, machines are everywhere in the modern city, and there are few or no shrines. Many fears are absent, there are hopes for further changes, there is much disposition to rely upon cooperation to effect the changes — to lessen the confusion, to clean the air, to improve the gardens. Yet there appears to be at least as much restlessness, for in the place of the ancient faiths and fears there is a continuous promise-making, a persistent demand for new satisfactions. The transfer of power from divinities to humans would not have made the modern crowds more obviously at peace with themselves than we suppose those tempestuous mortals were as they swarmed around Antony and Cleopatra throned beside the harbor. Playing with such suppositions we are touching upon the main question — what are the effects upon our living of our new-found power and autonomy, our new confidence, and our new uncertainties?

The postulate that science has all within its power encourages the belief that power is all that humans need not only in order to survive but to underwrite whatever sense of purposeful existence we continue to hold to. For we do hold to a sense if not a conviction of purpose beyond that of asserting power, we continue to ask questions that some science and some philosophy say it is pointless to ask — "Where am I, or what? From what causes do I derive my existence, and to what condition shall I return? Whose favor shall I court, and whose anger must I dread?"

In recent years some who repeat Hume's questionings have drawn the inference for themselves that all is absurd since the idea of meaning is absurd, and paradoxically they propose this formulation as a comfort, arguing that we have no choice but to live with a paradox and a contradiction. Existentialists have followed thought that leads this way and some of these have succeeded by various means in rejecting the modes of despair. Phenomenologists have discovered other means of accommodating human aspirations to a desacralized world, yet the empirical, purely secular views continue to make persuasive claims to adequacy.

In the midst of the variety and complexity of these movements one must be extremely diffident in claiming that one or another is in the ascendant or promises to dominate the others, but I think it is not wrong to say that for many years now positivism has been of extraordinary importance, and that scientists, social scientists, philosophers and artists have founded much of their work on grounds that only positivism would allow. I believe it is true that the postulates supporting this philosophy are increasingly vulnerable, and the allied reasonings that would reduce all that exists to physical elements are being modified in the theories of physicists,

13

among others, but whatever the directions and the conclusions of philosophy and criticism we must continue to believe that positivism will continue to sustain theory and experiment and the cult of power for a long while. The premises may ultimately be shown to be mistaken but they still serve to lead to results that may be validated otherwise.

The effort of positivistic science universally is to obtain knowledge that is at once explanatory and predictive. It looks towards the forming of theories which are presented as no more than descriptive generalizations, pointing to the regularity of the appearances and occurrences under observation. When the generalizations are accurate enough they imply a continuing regularity that becomes the basis for prediction. It is the resolution to exclude any conceivably metaphysical interest that justifies the negative character Leslie Kolakowski attributes to the positivist approach, as "a collection of prohibitions concerning human knowledge, intended to confine the name 'knowledge' or 'science' to the results of those that are observable in the evolution of the modern sciences of nature."[1]

Yet whatever illuminations and discoveries positivism has provided they have not persuaded all that the exclusion of metaphysics is other than a fatal defect. The thought continues to devil many that there must be some manner of study and instruction that will be of use to humans who are unable to think of themselves solely in the mechanical terms positivism tolerates. Strangely, even devoted scientists may conceive of their work as purposeful and as potentially if not inherently directed to good. This more often than not comes down to the intention to impress an ever vaster power into the service of humans, with the understanding that this is owing to us. Our scientists and especially our social scientists and those following after them — the consumers of the consumer society — may be falling back on naive and unworthy arguments to support the belief that we are entitled to survive and rule and prosper, for on reflection we find that what we are depending on is as insubstantially founded as a dream: "That there ought to be through all future time such a world fit for human habitation, and that it ought in all future time to be inhabited by a mankind worthy of the human name, will be readily affirmed as a general axiom or a persuasive desirability of speculative imagination (as persuasive and undemonstrable as the

14

proposition that there being a world at all is 'better' than there being none): but as a *moral* proposition, namely, a practical *obligation* toward the prosperity of a distant future, and a principle of decision in present action, it is quite different from the imperatives of the previous ethics of contemporaneity; and it has entered the moral scene only with our novel powers and range of prescience."[2]

The defenders of the humanities are not commonly prepared to counter the attractions of the sciences in their treating with human matters although serious efforts are being made continually even though, it seems, too often as rear guard actions. On the one hand, in forwarding what is called secular humanism, these studies are said to respond to the need to resist dogma in any form, whether offered in the name of religion or of science. The humanities, it is argued, provide the best means for the emancipation of thought and for supporting a rightful confidence in the unlimited power of criticism. With whatever claims, however tenuous, literature and philosophy and history and the fine arts can make to comprehensive meanings, the reasoning they exploit must be employed in examining and weighing the postulates and undertakings of the sciences, for all are partners in a common enterprise. So Michael Polanyi puts the case: ". . . scientific value must be justified as part of a human culture extending over the arts, laws and religions of man, all contrived likewise by the use of language."[3]

The other chief argument for the humanities harmonizes with this but only partly. Here the defenders say that poetry and philosophy and history support and even help substantiate the truths arrived at in the sciences. Philosophy and the arts may provide insights into reality and truth not normally within the range of scientific methods. The arts continually make known experiences and prospects that extend the reference of the hypotheses of science, so that literature and philosophy at least — Shakespeare and Plato, say — cooperate with the undertakings of science in exploring the possibilities of the infinite. The same point is made when someone asks whether the conceptions of Thales and Lucretius, of Bruno and Darwin, depend finally upon a combining of imagination and metaphysics with what comes under the head of observation and analysis.

Both arguments can be all but lost in a complex of issues, not least those that come forward when the suggestion is made that the sciences themselves are limited by their origins in something as mysterious as experience itself. But in any event, however to be regarded, these arguments are not currently making much headway for a variety of reasons, although in the end they may conclude in some success. There is still another argument, however, which may be the weakest of all intrinsically, but which is rather more attended to. This is chiefly put forward by practitioners in the arts and certain philosophers who say that the arts introduce us to the world of transcendent being and free us from illusion. In its various forms this reasoning derives from philosophies one may generally characterize as gnostic. The manifestos of surrealists, for example, declare that poetry and the arts in their inspiration and in their effect are modes of participation in a comprehensive consciousness, an immersion that enjoins the subversion of consciously ordered social arrangements in the interest of wholly new forms for human life. This and similar movements are of enormous influence, but insofar as they remain apart from institutions and particularly from educational institutions and are not determining their organization they enter only indirectly into debates on curricula. When their forwarders do ally themselves to political movements they of course help define revolutionary programs, but relying as much as they do on the non-rational and the irrational they are largely excluded from debates which depend upon traditional means of discourse. Accordingly, as long as this remains so, the claims for the humanities will continue to be made primarily in resisting or qualifying the authority of the sciences, and on other grounds than gnosticism would authorize.

Then there are those who identify themselves with the romantics in attempting to counter the desperate implications they find in granting science the authority it has attained. Throughout the schools and in the places of entertainment, works of literature and the other arts are said to have a saving power, even, I think, the equivalent to a sacramental power. Art like passion — "the holiness of the heart's affections" — illustrates the presence of the sacred, of what is to be honored at all costs, the holiness of the blind energies released in our cells and in the urgings of the unconscious. Whatever is exciting, the argument goes, is good, an

16

end in itself, and a sufficient end. And just as extremely, the claim is made for humanistic studies generally, that all that exploits sensibility, the greatest and the slight — the Bible, Shakespeare, the Pre-Raphaelites — testifies to the force of the energies waiting to be released in the race, and testifies that this is all the truth we need to know, life at its freest.

As I see it, much here is subterfuge, an effort to escape meeting metaphysical questions as such. Keats and so many of us are taking refuge in sensibility as a replacement for meaning, denying the claims of rationality as empirical science itself does but unlike science attaching to the messages of the senses the values properly belonging to other systems. The social sciences, in their turn, also commonly count on something like purity of intention, some inherent kindness, in the mind of the scientist and probably in the matter of his study, life itself. It would be much better if the defenders of the humanities as well as scientists appealing to humanitarianism would give up the claims for a wholly civilizing influence, and would say that all arts, not only those of the technologists, may distort, impoverish, and even nullify the will to live.

But one hardly needs wait for the *coup de grâce* from the irrationalists for whatever the right uses of the humanities they are now lending themselves to their own undoing. The methods followed by the sciences have had such impressive results that literary and historical studies have appropriated them for their own, in order, presumably, to obtain the respect paid to science. For example, stories about the gods in Homer are to be understood as embodying the principles governing the developments of society among the Greeks. Homer thus becomes the handmaid of sociology and anthropology however much Nietzsche and Jane Harrison thought it would be the other way around. The first chapter of *Genesis* is to be read as the manifestation of the structural patterns of the human mind. It becomes a text supporting the psychology of Piaget and the anthropology of Lévi-Strauss. The tragedies of Racine are crystallizations of the tensions introducing the seventeenth century into the revolutionary ferment of the modern age. They become footnotes documenting the Marxist hypotheses. The claims of science and of scientific method to take over the study of the humanities are indeed so persuasive that many of us are surprised to come upon Émile Brehier's re-

17

minder that the interminglings of Greek and Latin and Christian thought that have given form to our civilization cannot be disentangled, and that with the banishing of religion — "from the city" is his phrase — the humanities must also be banished. Insofar as the scientific methods pursued in the study of humane subjects are those sustained by analyses put to the service of the sciences, when they are supported by the postulates of positivism — as the methods of analysis currently almost always are — they do indeed dissipate any value the humanities possess apart from those reinforcing the discoveries of the sciences. The assumptions of positivism exclude from consideration any suggestion that the claim of the humanities to respect depends on the survival of philosophies agreeable to such support as in earlier times religion gave to the support of the humanities.

This is to say that humane study becomes primarily illustrative — historical, sociological, and psychological — and the content of the works studied is referred to other than their acknowledged intentions. There are of course many undertakings exploring aesthetic as well as philosophic considerations, particularly in the analysis of symbols. But humane studies in general have become all but exclusively analytic and descriptive, referring the works in question to external frames of reference in order to establish their significance. They aim at detachment and objectivity, and are neither morally nor dogmatically informed. They hereby take their place with other investigations pursued as sciences, which means usually as sciences are pursued in following the postulate that facts are the only possible objects of knowledge.

The issues are complex and an appeal to ancient pieties is obviously inadequate. The issues center on the strangeness of our present circumstances, on what we take to be the lack of coherence with the past. Our powers over nature now being what was hitherto unimaginable, all else partakes of this novelty. It is but a short time such power has been ours, and changes proceed so steadily that we hardly know what to set for a course. But the fact that we are conscious of this instability informs us of one thing, that this is the necessary condition of those who accept power as the one good. And with this recognition goes another, that our present circumstances can differ only in degree, not in kind, from those prevailing before. A perfected determinism that authorizes our entire subjection to the rule of things does not differ essentially from any fatalism that excludes the ultimate supremacy of divine powers. The enormous difference is in the more comprehensives promises of success, not for some exceptional Prometheus but for infinite numbers of persons, and for an infinitely more pervasive power and control than the Titan aimed for.

And in noting these differences we learn that the effects upon individuals' lives and dispositions, as well through what takes place in managing power as in what occurs through submission to it, cannot be otherwise than those told of in the stories of Lucifer and Alexander and so many others. The opportunities we now have, our invasions into the infinitesimal as into the vast, harnessing the energy of atoms and effecting cosmic changes, light up the confusion in which we are asserting our capacity to judge freely and to arrange our own affairs. Seeing that the universe we are endeavoring to take over reveals new vastnessess at every exploration we are apprised of our own inexpugnable limitations. Finding ourselves mites, we must conclude that our concerns are correspondingly diminutive. Our ambitions have thus led us to turn against ourselves, and what commenced as promising satisfactions beyond our wildest dreams ends in the approach to the void the existentialists have called our attention to.

To take this lead in an effort to establish a direction for education would be confessedly self-defeating. It thus appears that our ambitions themselves are self-defeating, and accordingly we are induced to look elsewhere for the decent sustaining of our hopes. And first and last, to turn to what positivists must ignore, that which is not observable — communication.

II

As I see it, the apologia for the humanities begins with an assessment of the value we attach to the delight humans take in communication for this delight is at the heart of our interest in reading literature as it is of our attention to all the arts, but it is in the arts that make use of speech and writing that we are best able to appreciate the character of what we mean by communication. Richard Hooker put it splendidly:

"Between men and beasts there is no possibility of sociable communion, because the well-spring of that communion is a natural delight which man hath to transfuse from himself into others, and to receive from others into himself especially those things wherein the excellency of his kind doth most consist. The chiefest instrument of human communion therefore is speech, because thereby we impart mutually one to another the conceits of our reasonable understanding. And for that cause seeing beasts are not hereof capable, forasmuch as with them we can use no such conference, they being in degree, although above other creatures on earth to whom nature hath denied sense, yet lower than to be sociable companions of man to whom nature hath given reason; it is of Adam said that amongst the beasts 'he found not for himself any meet companion.' Civil society doth more content the nature of man than any private kind of solitary living, because in society this good of mutual participation is so much larger than otherwise. Herewith notwithstanding we are not satisfied, but we covet (if it might be) to have a kind of society and fellowship even with all mankind. Which thing Socrates intending to signify professed himself a citizen, not of this or that commonwealth, but of the world. And an effect of that very natural desire in us (a manifest token that we wish after a sort an univeral fellowship with all men) appeareth by the wonderful delight men have, some to visit foreign countries, some to discover nations not heard of in former ages, we all to know the affairs and dealings of other people, yea to be in league of amity with them: and this not only for traffick's sake, or to the end that when many are confederated each may make other the more strong, but for such cause also as moved the Queen of Saba to visit Solomon; and in a word, because nature doth presume that how many men there are in the world, so many gods as it were there are, or at leastwise such they should be towards men."[4]

It is certainly true that "such conversation as soul to soul affordeth" in the course of a life counts for more than conversation between a man and a book, more even than the imagined conversation in which the singer of a song dreams of engaging the love of

20

an ideal audience, or of God, more than his sense of sharing the very life of magnificent beings as he sees that enacted upon a stage. Yet it appears that a certain disengagement of the reader in the act of reading, at once absorbed and detached, encourages particularly enrichening reflection — "a certain temperance in the very whirlwind of passion." He is being reminded of the character of his own life, an infinite variety of the thoughts and impulses of his own being start before him even as he is being charmed and carried away by the words of another. There is in this experience a value of still another kind than in the conversation of souls, a value men require for their fullest enjoyment of themselves, for the fullest uses of understanding, for he may take time to dwell upon what he is hearing, return again and again to the same text, renew the context. And this reflection, informed by the work he is intent on, tells him that the principles ordering the experience and the expression of another are the same as those at work within his own nature and understanding and language. The words of a stranger, from another time and place, from another culture, he judges, are not only such as might have been his, they might have been anyone's, and the pleasure of the recognition is partly in the knowledge of the sharing, and more meaningfully still in the marvel that this could ever occur.

Put in this way, to a sceptic the words might seem to deserve no serious attention whatever, and it would certainly be folly and worse to appeal to sensitivity as authority for them, the appeal must be to "truth" — and this time it is Petrarch who puts the matter in terms that lead the assertion into a generality: "In God's name, could you find a single word in these verses that would not be appropriate not only to Christians but to all men and all nations?" In the delight in recognizing our own thoughts, our own inmost thoughts, the very conclusions our living has led us to, in the words of a stranger, perhaps someone long since dead, each of us discovers, we infer, the experience of all men. In this delight we are affirming not only the quality of our individuality but of our humanity.

At this point the appeal of the speaker, the writer, the artist, the reader, is being made to the disposition we have to recognize what is common in the experience of each. And so the question re-forms itself: Is anyone ignorant of the peculiar need for and the peculiar satisfaction of communication? It seems obvious that the answer to this is no, and all that remains if we are to divine Hooker's and Petrarch's implied argument is to explore the significance of the delight we take, for example, in hearing Macbeth's

> Tomorrow and tomorrow and tomorrow
> Creeps in this petty pace from day to day;

in hearing Socrates,

> Then I say truly, Polus, that neither you nor I nor any man would rather do than suffer injustice;

in reading Huck Finn's

> You don't know about me without you have read a book by the name of *The Adventures of Tom Sawyer,* but that ain't no matter. That book was made by Mr. Mark Twain and he told the truth, mainly. There was things which he stretched, but mainly he told the truth. That is nothing. I never seen anybody but lied one time or another, without it was Aunt Polly or the Widow, or maybe Mary. Aunt Polly — Tom's Aunt Polly, she is — and Mary, and the Widow Douglas is all told about in that book, which is mostly a true book, with some stretchers as I said before.

And then one must take further steps, making it clear that it is not the satisfaction of feeling, the stirring of pleasure, or, in the most sustained and involved experience, excitement or enthusiasm or frenzy — whatever the intents, and effects, of Stravinsky and Giotto and Euripides — that gives this delight its final character and value. We need to demonstrate that the delight finally is not simply in sympathy but in understanding, it being understanding more than feeling that is moulding our participation in the life and the very way of life of another who yet remains another — it is in the reading of a book, in the joy of dancing, in the intent gaze, as it is in love and in devotion.

So persuaded we know we must bring reason to our help in rejecting all that would discountenance this trust and this delight — and we remember the charming remark of Malebranche, "I owe Descartes, or his way of philosophizing, the opinions that I oppose to his as well as my boldness in reproving them."

22

The delight we take in the company of others, in conversation and in all that the fellowship of language brings with it, are the joys of the senses and the imagination and sympathy as well as of the understanding. A definition would too much limit the character of this companionship, this sharing of thought and hopes and beliefs, of convictions, and perhaps even of life itself. Just as it has been said that an infant dies that has not been smiled on, so with us the need for company and for words and for the life and light in the thoughts of others. And again and again the delight is crowned with the confirmation of our reasonings about the world, our insights into truth, and with the confirmation of our moral sense. In apprehending what it is we share with others and with all that language lends us our understanding and our convictions deepen. We find ourselves looking more deeply or freshly into the rightness and wrongness of the courses we and others are following. We find our sense sharpened to the fineness or coarseness of certain manners. We become better acquainted with the ways of perfection.

This, one may say, everyone knows, and yet such are the persuasions of analysis and logic that in recent times many have come to doubt that communication is ever realized. A movement in thought developing in the seventeenth century, leading to the most impressive successes in science and technology, led through the same processes to a view of the minds of humans so isolated each from the other that no bridges can join them, and certainly not words in all their instability. Yet what everyone depends on, and so often to certifiable advantage, it must be possible to account for, and so again and again we are led to review the circumstances that have made for this impasse, to discover what we may retain from the revolutions of thought that have had this as one of their effects and learn what we may properly make of the confidence that is indispensable. Although the words are clumsy we are grateful for Merleau-Ponty's formulation he partly owes to Hegel, that the philosophic mission of the twentieth century is to explore the irrational and integrate it in a "larger" rationality.[5]

In antiquity and the Middle Ages confidence in the success of communication withstood the challenges of scepticism that have since all but triumphed. In the Renaissance there was the effort, even as the national cultures flowered, to make explicit universal

standards for theory and judgment and to refine a common language, most particularly for the ruling classes, using Greek and Latin writings as the basis of education. The faith seemed secure, that humans, endowed with reason, had access to the knowledge of the laws of nature and of nations. The schools would accommodate ancient to Christian teachings.

When we look over Professor Ronald Crane's survey of writers on education in the Renaissance we notice how assuredly they counted on the subscription of their readers, even though, with hindsight, we may see signs of the spiritual void that was preparing. There is Vives, for example, asserting that the classics "restore man to humanity and raise him towards God." Sir Philip Sidney rehearses commonplaces to demonstrate that works of literature and even dramas lead to self-knowledge and provide instruction in right-doing. Sir Thomas Elyot was assured that the classics were invaluable in teaching the young "to chew the cud of thought," that they helped boys to become prudent, just and temperate men, and worthy magistrates. Milton showed how they helped men perform skillfully and magnanimously both the public and private offices of peace and war, they helped them to establish the primacy of principle, and they sustained them in the courageous performance of their duties.

And so into recent times. For Cardinal Newman the classics were of inestimable worth in inducing a philosophic habit of mind and accordingly in enabling men to see their particular situations in perspective. For Matthew Arnold the classics led to a harmonious expansion of all the powers that contribute to the beauty and goodness of humans. In our own country Walter Lippman and Lewis Mumford have insisted on the need for the knowledge of great literature in enabling men to preserve the values of civilization, in resisting the ever-threatening return to barbarism: letters are the means of our communication with the greatest minds of the past; through study we join in a larger and larger community, we learn what we must measure up to, we obtain the benefits of instruction, and are better able to fulfill our responsibilities.

Petrarch had no doubt of his own reality, that he had true knowledge of himself and his humanity. The grounds were sure that justified him in the belief that he shared his idol Cicero's inmost feelings and thoughts — believing, also, that Cicero had anticipated his. On his part Cicero had reasoned his way through

to an idea of the human constitution which in philosophic language he thought of as *essence.* Communication came about through a sharing of essence, a common stuff as it were, joint participation in a reality which was itself a bond between the mind in understanding and what was understood. Essence, it has been said, was the El Dorado of centuries, and what Petarch affirmed was an almost universal reference. Recently, in Michael Polanyi's adaptation, we come upon reasoning that renews something of the earlier assurance: ". . . knowledge and reality are tied together by a natural affinity of structure — by the bond of *connaturalitas,* as the Scholastics had it. Knowledge by its very nature is a process, better still an aspiration directed toward an anticipated goal and at the same time an orderly rise from one level of vision to a higher one. The meshing of this intellectual endeavor consists in the disclosure of reality. But reality, independent though it is of our knowing it, owns a peculiar fitness for becoming known by us. Its own hierarchical structure both parallels and renders possible the cognitive enterprise of man. His intellectual pursuit appears to be prefigured by the stratification of reality."[6] Language and all its works play their parts in this binding.

Now, of course, education has abjured the support of such reasoning, but it is clear that we need to re-discover the means of relating "the knower to the known" in such ways as will sustain the sense of purpose we continue to depend on, that will unite the rational with the irrational, that we may square our thought with our living.[7]

The methods of technology so successful in the material world are now at work in manipulating natural and mental processes, developing attitudes it is accurate to speak of as dehumanized. The reasonings of many philosophers also have as radically undermined the confidence that as humans we possess constant, distinguishing virtues. We are as much cut off from the past with respect to ruling ideas as in the conditions of daily life. We employ all the time-honored words only to call them empty. We are prevented from appealing to a common understanding of what is "real;" probability has replaced certainty as the goal of aspiration; the idea of the meaningful is abandoned. We sometimes discern but nebulous differences between humans and animals, we may not with assurance distinguish between Greeks and

25

Barbarians, between the rational and the irrational. What has taken the status of received ideas among philosophers and social scientists has become the conventional wisdom in the schools and in the practicing of the arts. As one of the consequences language itself is (elaborately) misprized by Becket, Ionesco, Wittgenstein. Nothing is left of the golden world of Essence but the shells of words.

And yet, ironically, so many of those who insist that the world and the human mind are alike dilapidated unite in insisting that their audiences concur when they assert that any meaning is tautological, or that everything is absurd. They appear to believe that all experience will bear them out even though that expectation involves an assumption they are not entitled to, that at bedrock all humans do possess a common character only if that be the capacity to attest to the one reality, the void.

When we hear Camus' Mersault say he "finally understood that nothing was of any importance whatever" we understand that the novelist is soliciting not only an audience but a following. He is counting upon the same use for fellowship the early humanists celebrated even in proposing the negation of its worth. The one most tangled in the paradox, I think, is Sartre, although no one is more obdurate in clinging to the possibility of dignity. But so effective have been the arguments that there are no bonds to bridge the consciousness and understanding of individual humans that *angst* and despair are accepted by many as the human condition. Isolation is complete. Sartre acknowledges this with horror and when led to characterize love, what he comes up with is "the absurd conflict between two liberties that vainly seek to grow apart and at the same time to submit to fascination."[8] It is most curious that speculation should so insistently contradict what experience so constantly affirms, and with passion normally only within the capacity of believers.

It is the conviction of the intrinsically important and the open acknowledgment of inherent worth that have guided traditionalists, inspired education, and sustained the claims of society for centuries, and it is precisely such that has become anathema to the forwarders of the main directions in philosophy. This is also excluded from the concerns of those who use the postulates that have succeeded so well in the physical sciences as guides in the study of human matters. Customarily acknowledging no debt to metaphysics, to these the very idea of humanity is blurred, and as it is with behaviorists the study of humans is confined within the same limits operable in the study of animals. It is true that Marxists, phenomenologists, and existentialists have need of an idea of the distinctively human, and neo-scholastics and idealists continue to offer supporting doctrines. There are also among artists those who undertake to sustain the ancient allegiances. But it is not only linguistic analysts and reductionists in general who have brought these schools into discredit, it is almost all who are bound to the example of Descartes, drawn to rely only on mathematics and the knowledge deriving from that, which in the end points to such mechanical systems as are thrown up by the universe or as can be invented.

Scientific methods, of course, were never supposed to certify meanings. By their character they are fitted to take into view only such bonds allying humans to each other as are to be inferred in mechanical relations. Yet the awesomeness of the physical changes technology has effected — in genetics, in lunar landings, and so much else — has had effects upon our attitudes as remarkable, as unsettling, as the orientations sustaining the theorizing that made them possible. Since objective study has been so effective in these realms the temptation is all but irresistible to propose that the mechanical manipulation that it authorizes may be as effective in controlling humans as in controlling other material configurations.

Further, since matter itself makes no claim upon us other than through the appeals of abstraction and generalization, and these bear no reference to inherent quality, or indeed to "reality," so the manipulations are guided by interests that may not properly be referred to meaningful intent, and are simply those of the technician. The fact that reasoning on these matters generally make reference to "man" rather than to "men" shows the extent to which the general and abstract dominate this thinking. The notion of individuality is too refractory for the purpose, and thus the belief in the impersonal functioning of the human is reinforced.

And now sophistication takes over: the dimension common to matter and life and consciousness is motion. As matter finds forms in the operations of machines, thought seeks its way in the formalizations of logic that correspond to the regularities observable in mechanics. Language plays its part in this operation as word-games. In the idea of game the idea of communication as delusion is inherent. This follows since all living beings by definition are without essential, constant features. Yet because the games are being played, and played out, by those who use language, it is obvious that something is passing for communication, and the effort must be made to explain what is taking place.

It is clear that no construction reductionists devise can account for the satisfaction the classical tradition honors in praising the delight letters and the arts and conversation afford. These are effects informed not only with the conviction of communion but also upon the conviction of truths and of the sharing of them. Deprived of such support it is in a kind of desperation that descriptions of behavior are offered as demonstrating concurrence in understanding. There are, for example, those who administer Rorsach tests to natives of the islands of Alor, and they conclude from these that individuals still in the Stone Age may master modern machines. They go on to conclude from further tests that with respect to language "approximate translations" are effected, "for the diversity of understanding is not irreducible."[9]

Fair enough if this is left as a descriptive statement, but it should be obvious that as a statement accounting for communication it is question-begging — "diversity" being so loose a catchall one cannot know the character and extent of any agreement these beings are supposed to have reached. True agreement on matters touching men's business and bosoms depends on the conviction of identical experience within the diversity. In London recently a Zulu company put on an exhilarating production of *Macbeth* in their own language and in native dress, and one of the startling effects came in Lady Macbeth's projection of those tensions we have long understood to be appropriate to the guilt-ridden in the northern, Christian world. The foreign audience perceived in the otherwise exotic Lady not an "approximate translation" but the authentic re-creation of experience it knew for its own. Whatever passed between the performers and the audience was no figuring-forth of ink-blots offered for comparison.

One of the ways to get at the issues it is necessary to resolve is in examining the particular conditions involved in the growth of the sceptical movement.

The reductionist analysis of human activities ends in descriptions by observers who in the terms of the undertaking ignore their own concerns when noting and classifying the experiences and values of others. This procedure now sanctioned in so many areas was first perfected in the study of matter and nature when the idols of metaphysics had been exorcised, that is to say, when certain remarkable initiatives in philosophic speculation provided the necessary attitudes that allowed for it. The direction philosophy took remains of the first importance in the current practice of all the sciences, and it is helpful to keep the chief landmarks in mind through however bare a recounting.

Nicholas of Cusa commenced his speculation, as Cassirer put it, not in asking about God, but in asking about the possibility of the knowledge of God. The crucial step had been taken: reasoning is to be directed through exploring the faculties and capacities of the individual. The way is opened into what is to be called subjectivity.

Bruno followed. Like Nicholas he held to the idea of an all-encompassing cosmic order but he went on to claim authority for the individual reason in discovering the individual's place in that order. He is advancing further in the argument that Descartes will bring to a decisive conclusion — in the end thinking finds its sanction in the existence of the thinking self, in the discovery of that, not in discovering the relation of the self to the encompassing universe.

Then the time came, with Locke and Berkeley and Hume, for the denial not only of the possibility of certain knowledge but of the existence of the self that reveals the grounds of all uncertainty. And so, finally, Hume's protestation: "For my part when I enter most intimately into what I call *myself,* I always stumble on some particular perception or other, of heat or cold, light or shade, love or hatred, pain or pleasure. I never can catch *myself* at any time without a perception, and never can observe anything but the perception. When my perceptions are removed for any time, as by sound sleep, so long am I insensible of *myself,* and may truly be said not to exist. And were all my perceptions removed by death, and could I neither think, nor feel, nor see, nor love, nor hate after the dissolution of my body, I should be entirely annihilated, nor do I conceive what is further requisite to make me a perfect non-entity."[10]

It follows, grotesquely enough, that there can be no communication between nonentities. The phrasing of Bachelard sets the seal on this condition: "the world in which we live is not the world in which we think."

Thus the picture takes form of Hume himself calling out, saying — what turns out not to be true — that no one hears him:

> "I am first affrighted and confounded with that forlorn solitude in which I am placed in my philosophy, and fancy myself some strange uncouth monster, who, not being able to mingle and unite in society, has been expelled all human commerce, and left utterly abandoned and disconsolate. Fain would I run into the crowd for shelter and warmth; but cannot prevail with myself to mix with such deformity. I call upon others to join me, in order to make a company apart; but no one will harken to me. Every one keeps at a distance, and dreads that storm which beats upon me from every side."[11]

It is precisely this cry we do hear, that the reductionists themselves take up and join in with. And then, as if some malevolence in logic itself were at work, void calling out to void, falling back upon some unidentifiable energy in consciousness, the genii of matter that form matter into machines, interpreted in the terms of materialism and empiricism, take over from the idols of the essentialists. The enticements of mechanicism now subdue us, overcoming the scepticism that urged Descartes on in the name of rationality. And so his descendants — Freud and Marx and Pavlov — it is well said, "killed him." "In order to make way for modern man, for man as science sees him, it was necessary to liquidate the *cogito*. To kill Descartes."[12]

Reductionist reasoning has taken various casts — positivism, behaviorism, determinism — but whatever the emphasis there is agreement upon this, that the self as a superior, rational being dissolves in non-being. The fact of consciousness continues to cause problems, and especially this one, that what has been reduced to a nonentity should be conscious of "itself." The hoped-for solutions are of two orders — either that, when analysis is still more refined, consciousness will be shown to be material, or else, by the very fact that it resists measurement it is proper to ignore it: "The best way to deal with consciousness or introspective, subjective experience in any form, . . . is to ignore it. Inner feelings and thoughts cannot be measured or weighed; they cannot be centrifuged or photographed, chromatographed, spectrographed, or otherwise recorded or dealt with objectively by any scientific methodology. As some kind of instrospective, private, inner something, accessible only to the one experiencing individual, they simply must be excluded by policy from any scientific model or scientific explanation."[13]

The more analytical procedures succeed in disposing of questionable inferences the more difficult it becomes to account for anything like communication — the conclusions of positivism are clear. In a typical characterization: Matter has evolved into life and then into thought by successive mutations in a continuing process. Humans are of the same quality as all the rest, and their distinction from other matter is accidental only, the individual's consciousness of his actions and his internal dispositions. But in the end all this is to be referred to biological activities that are in turn referred to physics and chemistry, these in turn reducible to the movements of machines. "The social sciences lose their last flexibility when they coordinate their studies with psychoanalysis and theories of the subconscious, which close every loophole to the possibility of free human action, and hopefully seal up the entire undertaking in the terms of perfected determinism."[14]

From another aspect, it is said that behaviorist and positivist science regard the human animal not as an articulate being calling for intelligent responses from his fellows but as a largely unconscious emitting center, the noises having no other value than those of a buoy with a bell on, moved passively by the swell of the encompassing sea.

There are other implications to the paradox for it appears that these materials that give rise to consciousness and thought also give witness to a certain constancy in the individual's own existence, and to ideas implicit in his consciousness of his liberty to judge and his power to certify. Hume judges himself to be freely arriving at truths. And so even with the very instruments of scepticism one will sooner or later discover the sceptics themselves depending on what by their own terms is not to be certified. The point has been put well: "It is essential and central to the notion of a person that there be noncriterial knowledge of personal identity. For something to lack altogether the ability to have this kind of knowledge of itself would be for it to lack a kind of memory the possession of which seems essential to being a person, namely the ability to remember particular events and actions in the past."[15] Hume himself admitted in the Appendix to his *Treatise* he had not been able "to explain the principles, that unite our successive perceptions in our thought or consciousness." The point is that Hume and Bachelard *know* they are living in divided worlds, a knowledge they can only refer to the existence of a self enduring time, the present itself known as the embodiment of the past.

Descartes himself defined a kind of memory that enabled him to conceive of his existence in the world — "no one can be sure he thinks and exists if first he does not have knowledge of what it is to think and exist."[16] Reasoning thus he is thinking back to his remembrance of somewhat in his early consciousness that he must appeal to in validating what he is now making of his thought. Hume wrote an account of his own life, shaping in words and syntax the identity that took form and that he came to own. This disposition to look back, which normally means to look back to childhood, is more than an attempt to sketch an account of the history of one's life, the details and the sequences — the motive runs much deeper, it is to discover the right to claim validity for thought.

In short, the escape from metaphysics has not been successful. And I believe it is when we give our attention to what this "looking back" signifies, what the appeal to remembrance entails, that we are able to embark upon the reasoning that will counter the reductionists successfully, and that will lead to the right valuing of what the humanities offer.

"Memory is the mother of the Muses, offering the light we seek out to illuminate our present."

To paraphrase Georges Gusdorf: In the life of the individual mental and spiritual habits take form just as physiological and muscular habits do, through repetition. The past incorporates itself in us and becomes the gauge of the future. The past does not pass away, least of all for one so dedicated as a scientist must be, it is never erased but is converted into his very continuance. But the past is composed not only of the decisions he has made and the directions he has taken, it is also composed of his refusals — these, like the acceptances, being choices, preferences, valuings and disvaluings. He remains the ensemble of these through all their reorderings. All that he has been he consults as he treats with the present, there is a continual summing up as it were, in part consciously, in part through the habit his nature has taken, taking form as much as it suits him with words, but often also in but nascent thought. His effort continually is to serve his authentic being.[17]

The conclusion we might draw from the successes of a mechanistic view is that it is useless to appeal to "human nature" since the configurations of the particles that we are take but transient forms, forever disappearing, never repeated. We are never to think of the present as "incorporating the past," never consciously or unconsciously may we lay claim to continuity. This is as much as to say that *self*-consciousness has been obliterated, and if it were possible to be coherent in such a state it would be to say that all we know is perpetual strangeness. All undertakings then, the extension of power that science and technology always look towards, would be undirected, there being no reference in the past to take sights by — and this prospect is so murky the endeavors of science could not but die in being born.

In short, the denial of a continuing identity does in logic conclude in absurdity, and the implications that follow from this reveal what we instinctively responded to initially in observing the inconsistency in Hume's complaint. And at this point it becomes possible to give a hearing to the traditional humanists' proposition in asserting the fact of constants in the experience of humans.

"What if it could be proven that in time human beings will be utterly transformed, the faculty of reason itself altered in its modalities and intent on wholly other matters, and not only with respect to criteria for truth but with some wholly new idea of truth itself? There are philosophers among us who claim that the advances in our reasoning powers are not only leading us to new results but are changing the nature of reason itself. If this is true, then all of human life would be in a state of constant change, and the ones who would have the best understanding of what was taking place would be those whose humanistic training had accustomed them to compare the newest phases of thought with the most ancient."[18]

We know change only in knowing what has been changed.

Deprived of that knowledge we should be deprived of consciousness. But even though there are mechanists who suppose that that which is not measureable can be ignored, that consciousness can be ignored, it yet remains. As does memory. It is the memory of the past of others as well as of the individual self that is being called upon in examining the changes that do take place as well as those that thought projects and particularly that fanaticism projects. And particularly the fanaticism that derives from the conviction of a perfected determinism.

The uses of memory are not restricted to Freud's conclusions, for the role of conscious reflection is of equal importance with what manifests itself in the cells of the body. Rather, they are more significantly determined by the perception of parallels between the elements and orderings of the individual's being, with what language and the conventions of art acquaint him with in his people's and in the race's past. It is in the perception of the parallels with the human past that he understands what it is he takes as the valid form of his own living.

And yet, still entertaining a prospect of so many of the astonishing achievements — genetic development, mind-changing processes, computer calculations — that have followed upon such successful turnings of the mind outward, we are drawn to imagine ourselves newly created as monsters, which is to say as caricatures of ourselves, of what we know ourselves to be. And as always with the monstrous of our own making there is humor, and this reminds us that there is folly in relying upon precise and perfect predictability in human matters. As Popper insists, indeterminism is not enough, and a perfected determinism is more assuredly out of bounds. It is best, I think to hold with Émile Bréhier, that if humans are to lay claim to one virtue, it must be awe.[19]

III

Once a child is old enough he is sent to school. Models are set before him, the disposition to emulate — complex and in many ways unfathomable — is an incentive all count on. Quite as unfathomable and as unforeseeable are the experiences he will meet that provide the matter and direction for his growth, invitations to apply his capacities and to discover the shape and substance of what will be commitments.

The language he was born to, created no one knows how over the aeons, out of the needs and concerns and joys of generations, infinitely rich, is yet barely rich enough for his uses. He will find many right words, he will labor all his life long to find more, and he needs all the help he can get.

And so his elders provide him with texts — after the nursery rhymes and old wives' tales before he could read, the Bible, the Koran, legends and fantasies. And so he finds his way among them.

No one knows yet what he will make of all this, nor does he, nor will he ever, but the experiences of many will have set out traditions and a sustaining faith will select the indispensable. In the schools there will be serious efforts to divine the right stages of the child's initiation, and he himself — or better, his nature acting for him — will accept and reject as assimilation proceeds.

In a particular community it might be judged unthinkable for a boy to grow up without learning to revere Daniel Boone, a girl the children of *Little Women*. Elsewhere, as with the young ones of Faulkner's Mississippi, there will be stories of those closer home — men and women out of the turmoil of the war that much of the thought of those around him still centers on.

And then there will be sustained disciplines. A young Spaniard will read about El Cid, a young Frenchman in time about Polyeucte, children about the discovery of America. If tradition rather than politics is permitted to govern — instead of texts of Mussolini or Mao or Dr. Spock — texts the centuries have submitted to trial, then it will be as rich in form and matter as the deepest among them can take in. It will be no mere child's play, but it will also be child's play.

In the current disarray of thought the idea of a classic has lost almost all its force, but whenever a great work is put forward, stirring such appreciation as it does, all are moved to see within it much that we see in the world about us. When Telemachus set out to look for his father, we see ourselves making the same journey. As story after story that have interested so many are absorbed, the sense grows of sharing in the experience of a people, and sometimes of a race.

I have been speaking as if the most important ends of education could be served through translations. This is not so, for everyone's reflection depends upon such mastery over words as no translator can demonstrate. It is difficult to object to those who say that no language on earth can match Greek in supplying thought and sensibility with speech. But there is a more telling argument than Coomaraswamy offered against insisting on allowing it to dominate curricula — a decent acquaintance requires more time than a curriculum can afford. The essential remains, however, the needs for expression are such that the most sustained study of language employed nobly is indispensable. This may be one's own, although in general an apt pupil profits from the study of any strange language in undertaking to get hold of his own. For he very much needs to know that for all the likenesses between peoples there are differences that cannot be bridged, and the task of translation makes these evident as probably nothing else does for it points to relationships his own language and his own people have not made so much of, or in not the same way. Resolved not to accept substitutes he recognizes beauties he might never know otherwise —

Dans le fond des forêts votre image me suit —
words he foregoes translating, now taking for his own the alien sounds for what he might have thought ineffable. In another language the incantatory maintains an almost miraculous authority, the charm out-goes the sense, and like those guards in Sicily, freeing the prisoners who recited lines of Euripides for them, we set no limit on our prizing.

And so, in speaking of the humanities we know we must never get too far away from particulars, from the experience of particular assimilations and joys. Generalizations are necessary, leading as they do to such justifications as discourse may develop. Accordingly there is a special point, I believe, in recapitulating if not an individual experience one that may be representative, to keep before us the primary matter, that while words are common coins they are also the signs of the irreducible and the inviolable.

Through association with others humans from the time of birth grow into the assurance of character and purposeful direction that sustains our lives. An infant is fed and in return smiles at his benefactor. A child tumbles a pile of blocks and sets about reassembling them. He plays hide-and-seek with a stranger, an animal, his shadow. He finds himself endowed with words, with sentences, with dramas. He holds hands, he dances, he composes elaborate songs, singing in imagined ceremonies. His body masters innumerable skills, his eyes and ears discover infinite discriminations. And all the while, mind and body growing, his consciousness becomes articulate, words come forward in endless exclamation and conversation, addressed to himself, to the air, to the sky, to others, in waking and even in sleeping. These help him form the idea of himself the growth of his body and mind allows and favors "in the day's glorious walk and peaceful night," in vexation and pleasure, in the labor to conceive, in honoring and cherishing and playing.

Language becomes his all but everlasting dependency, as much his support and burden as arms and legs and eyes and ears — he is never so much alone that words do not stand by him. They can let him down, or the wrong ones or an insufficiency can, but as he grows he learns that it is not simply words, and not his invented sounds, or his peculiar thoughts, but the language itself, of his family, his people, and in the end of humanity that is accompanying and lighting up and directing his growth, the words in the ordered speech he has inherited from street-talk, from stories and songs, from all he cultivates. And this consciousness he has come to think of as his character, as himself, this growing sense of his as life endowed with sense and purpose, takes the final stamp of sanctity in his mind through the words he finds that do not betray what he has all the while been fostering, sensing that the value he sets upon his life derives from the faith that he is treating with truth, that his life is worthy insofar as in his thought and act he does not play false.

This is to offer but a brief characterization of the rudimentary activity that educational plans embody in more formal and sophisticated ways, plans in which education through letters — when sounds are transcribed — is the specially honored instrument enabling individuals to try their wings.

The dependence upon language is dependence upon the need for expression and fellowship and learning. In varying degrees utterance effects communication, with others immediately present, or only in thought. It is in the belief as well as in the success of communication that the individual finds himself strengthened in assurance, in the knowledge of what he is doing, even justified in predicting the consequences that may follow what he does. The assurance that he gains through his success in relating words to experience enables him to relate the interests that are important to him to those important to others even as, paradoxically, it is also the re-assurance of his individuality. He becomes the more certain of himself as he comes to understand his interests as generic, learning the right use of the language he has inherited.

As a child he conceives of a thousand forms for his life — as a frontiersman, a singer, an astronaut. He is no more absorbed in the sense of the person he is than of the innumerable lives that are never to be his. In all their variety they have names, they are pictured infinitely, in words and in stories. Again and again these exhilarating prospects and the choices that make them seem possible he relates to what he is hereby acknowledging as that which identifies him with other members of the race. No doubt some visions suit him better than others, and in the end, of course, he will be all of them as well as something quite different. In a wonderful way his playing with the sense of the strange and the generic enables him to know better the uniqueness of the form that is to be his own. Shakespeare's Pericles, buffeted by storms, forsaken time and again, yet persisted in his quite normal and necessary activities — laboring to survive, maintaining his loves, preparing for parenthood. He spoke the words that are in the back of everyone's mind in anticipating the future — speaking of himself as one "on whom perfection waits." Which is to say, as one for whom fortune or fate, however time's workings are conceived, is counted on to permit his right growth and flourishing. With Leonardo he believes that the universe is on the whole benevolent.

All of us, having found these or words like them, are strengthened as we would not otherwise be in resolving to make the best of circumstance. Coming upon the words Shakespeare or some other has given figurings in his thought we take them not only as those appropriate to that imaginary voyager but for our own, and we find ourselves, however much constrained already by the years we have passed through, once again believing we may so act that destiny will favor us.

The boy grows into the man.

The words of the Chorus in *Antigone* in making their magnificent boast are defining the capacities each human identifies as his own: "There are many marvels, but none more awesome than man. He traverses the hoary sea, driven by the south wind through surges that engulf him. The immortal, inexhaustible Earth, supreme among the gods, he wears away, turning up the soil with teams of horses, ploughing back and forth year after year. The skillful man ensnares and captures the careless flocks of birds, and the nations of wild beasts, and the briny race of the sea with the coiled meshes of his nets. With his engines he overcomes the wild beasts ranging the mountains, he tames the shaggy-necked horse with a yoke and the indomitable mountain bull.

"He has taught himself speech and winged thought and ways to rule a city. He has learned to escape the piercing cold and the rain storms under the open sky, he invents many duties. He never goes forward to meet what is to come without provision. Death alone he has not found a way to escape although he has discovered ways of curing all other illness."

The boy becomes a man while nature consults with his imagination. As adventures offer, as obligations take form, as possibilities are extinguished, he finds what it is he is living up to — as a hunter, a seaman, a builder. He may in the course of life meet with some to whom he responds in such admiration and sympathy that he is able to appreciate the skills and deeds and rewards their energies have led to. He learns from talk and from example. In the doings of the playground, the school, the beach, the public buildings, his imaginings come to square with circumstance, with the way things are and as they can be. He learns what the mountains are he is to scale, what seas to subdue, what humans he will measure himself by. He learns the rules of the game that is to be his.

As with those Sophocles' chorus sang of, so, for an example, we may imagine it was with the boy Orestes whose story so many of the ancient writings trace. His was to be a life of horror and glory, he would be matching wits with the greatest of his time and with fate. A child in our century will be more conscious of masses and organizations defining the labyrinth he must find his way in — Orestes could see the barriers and turnings more distinctly, knowing more surely the particular individuals he must treat with, forces that, as god-directed, he would know that all men reverenced. More surely than a modern child's his thought would be intent at every moment on the price exacted for commitment. And so, all that is strange to us in the very clarity in which Orestes sees the issues becomes the more impressive. In a dream Zeus commanded him to avenge his father, and he promised him he would not suffer for this. And so the vote that cleared Orestes on the Areopagus accorded with the will of Zeus.

"He who of his own will and without constraint follows righteousness shall not be unblessed, nor shall he perish." (Aeschylus, *Eumenides*, 544-5)

In pride and in accepting abasement he chose to live up to ideas he had formed of himself as a son, as an avenger, as the faithful observer of divine injunction. Such directions had been given him by all he had been taught in the stories of warriors and parents and kin and enemies, in what he came to know of his family's and his people's past, in their religion, their manners, in the testimony of their nobility and their ferocity.

For the sake of a betrayed and murdered father he would murder his mother and her lover. The Furies would pursue him. A friend and sister were indeflectibly loyal, and Argos itself held him as much in awe as in fear. But in hate as in love, in honor as in shame, in revenge as in piety, he was trapped, and it is a wonder he believed any freedom at all had been left to him.

When we look closer at the events of a life so unlike any we suppose might be ours we nevertheless come in time to find in the strange and sometimes repelling somewhat we suppose common to many others, some perhaps to the general human state. Reminded of events that took place before the crime we see that so much that took place in the past — matters Orestes could have had no knowledge of — were leading to entanglements there could have been no way for him to avoid. All of us as children have learned of the unavoidable, but what poetry, and especially from a strange world, provides us with is statements about particular causes, particular powers, that determine the inevitable, even giving these the names of gods. The strangeness and above all the reasonableness of this turns out to be a learning we cherish. The idea of ancient and even original causes takes on another wealth of meanings as we grow older, leading us to wonder we would not willingly forego.

Zeus knew in advance what others would learn after the fact, that if Aegisthus ignored his warning and in order to obtain Clytemnestra for his wife should slay Agamemnon, Agamemnon's son would avenge him. But what all at the time did also know was that every one of these driven creatures lived their lives in the shadow of the curse fallen upon the descendants of the house of Atreus. Enjoying whatever innocence had been granted him, Orestes, too, long before the horrible fulfillment, would have known of the coming darkness. We, too, in so different a setting, have known forebodings, and even, in all probability, have anticipated helplessness in the face of catastrophe.

He obeyed Zeus's bidding, and Athena would say that for what Clytemnestra had done it had been right for him to kill her. The terrible deed became a glorious example. At a later time she would remind Telemachus — "Hast thou not heard what fame goodly Orestes won from men in slaying his father's murderer, guileful Aegisthus? And thou, too, my friend, for I see that thou art fair and tall, must be valiant, that men yet to be born may speak well of thee." (*Odyssey,* I, 298-302)

However strange much of this is, I believe we understand that Orestes was faced with a choice he could not evade — honor to be obtained through crime, or disgrace if he allowed the shameless to prevail. He became the man it was possible for him to be in submitting to the powers that in cursing blessed him. In that obedience, the story tells us, he would attain such merit as would redeem the rest. When after many years he was released from the suffering the Furies exacted, he heard from Athena the words that would never have been his had he not fulfilled the awful duty: "for as the gardener, tending his plants with love, so I cherish most the unblighted of reverent men." (*Eumenides,* 910-11)

What Orestes' destiny had not marked out in all particulars he himself perfected through his capacity for resolution, his restless reasoning, the depth of his reverence. Much was his endowment as an Argive, much was done as it would have been by any son dishonored as he was, not only because Agamemnon was his father but also because he was so great a man, and it was greatness he was also honoring and must himself attain.

Just as we conceive that as a growing boy he would have mulled over what he had been learning of the life around him, as experience opened up and conditions set their terms upon his flourishing, so we, reading of him, in our minds put ourselves in his place. With our very different perspectives we assess what we ourselves would bring to bear faced with the same circumstances. We learn from his story much that in childhood we had learned from our playmates, from the friend who kept his promises, from those who failed us, from the bully and the sneak, from dirty tricks. Just as we learned of paths through the labyrinths of trust and distrust among children, so we figure what it meant for a cousin to plot against his cousin through his wife, and for that wife to become an accomplice in murder. We learn what it meant for a boy growing up, faced with shame, to labor to avert dishonor.

So with a boy from the Appalachians, stuffing a mandolin into his duffle bag, landing on an African shore, making up a song about a wife he had left — moving into the maelstrom of wars he would never comprehend, but as questionless in duty. As a child he had heard of feuds and houses and churches set afire, of detailed cruelties, of the ways of glory. And so everywhere imagination takes hold of images of horror and splendor as its native element, as the mysterious but certain foretelling of what is to come. Much he learns of from what had indeed happened, much from stories, and all become his sounding board.

In this stirring within ourselves of the recognitions of good and evil we are responding with much more than elementary sensations even though we may in time be persuaded to interpret these as configurations in the patterns of our nerves inherited with the rest of our bodies from our ancestors. We respond not only with our feelings but with what the words for good and evil bring with them, with what thought is teaching us about deeds and about our feelings towards them; with what words and thought alone certify and feeling itself cannot, the reality of the energies working toward our defilement and benediction. And from stories and fables such as these, from the records of history and from countless kinds of relations, we explore the reaches of our nature and our knowledge.

But the final use of the humanities comes through the fineness of the discriminations that are only within the province of art. Such as these in the *Odyssey,* delicacy and fineness and the appreciation of love that only the best find words for:

42

"Thus she spoke, and this made him wish even more to weep. And he cried as he held his well-pleasing wife in his arms. And as the sight of land causes swimmers to rejoice when Poseidon has smashed their well-built boat in the open sea. A few escape the hoary sea and swim to shore, their bodies crusted with brine. When they set foot on the beach they rejoice, having escaped such evil. So it was with her at the sight of her husband, and she would not let her white arms fall from his neck." (XXIII, 231-40)

Such grace as speech is equal to.

IV

When we pay respect to the uses of language and letters conceived of in this way we know we are considering the bridge that leads from wonder and sympathy to commitment. We are, it seems perforce, assessing the ways in which thought may be squared with what may be required of us in action.

Our own imaginings, the crowded worlds that even in talking to ourselves we give life to, may lack the significant pointings and the self-sufficiency that grace similar picturings when they are defined and disciplined by the principles governing rhetoric and the arts. Our own imaginings are like dreams in this, imbued with the air of fatality, and even when taking the forms of persons are yet deprived of the manner of creatures acting responsibly. And thus we value the more the figures and reasonings the arts reveal to us as possessing the fullness of being and the beauty belonging to the free. We take to them — Jean Valjean, Huck Finn, Cordelia — as to creatures to be prized as we prize our ideas of ourselves. They seem to tell us that all along our own thoughts and, more, the mysterious currents within consciousness, participate in such life as we perceive in the representations of art, that in their very formings they attest to the like impetus. Victor Hugo was so moved by the wealth of the Shakespearean creation that he burst out, "Some men are very oceans!" He saw here a power he could only liken to the source of life, the all-bearing sea. And in his very exclamation he signified the capacity of all of us to recognize the depths and richnesses that are also ours. The conceit itself leads us to compare what takes place in our imaginings and assessments of experience with what Shakespeare and all works of art acquaint us. The conceit is forced upon us as we consider the idea of coming-into-being, of forms and meanings taking form in thought, and of life taking form in the world about us.

Knowing it is a power in nature itself that is leading us we are happy in submitting our delight to the scrutiny of reflection and judgment, in this finding still more delight. And in the reflection as in the imaginings we discover that our experience comprehends more than we knew, or even guessed; we find ourselves becoming, as it were, more capacious, endowed with the insights and orderings of others as if it were we who had brought them forth. And as we entertain the visions of Homer and Archilochus, of Cimabue and Tintoretto, of Shakespeare and Mozart, as pageants and tapestries and songs are received by us, we come to see that it is the unending wealth of a universe.

We take to Hugo's conceit through the inclination to suppose that the life of our minds as that in the world arises out of an original stuff, a primordial matrix as it were. This inclination depends upon our disposition to relate being to dimension.

In following this conception we find ourselves trying to imagine the formless space out of which all this comes, vast reaches it would be absurd to speak of as existing within us if there were any other way of speaking — conceiving of the unconfinable as confined. Reflecting further we shall notice stirrings in the darkness, and the darkness lightening, and however uncoached our attention we commence to distinguish among the motions. We sense ourselves in the presence of an energizing power that gives form and quality to the semblances of things and persons. What at first may appear much like shadows in motion takes on substance and color and expression, as often as not figures such as those we know in life, but often also fantastic or monstrous. It is as if from within our natures, our cares — in reflecting after the fact we are able to speak in this way — are giving birth to the representations of physical things: the sense of time passing leads into the picture of a river in flood: space reaches out to walls; motion becomes the person of a woman dancing. We judge that it is with us as it was

44

with Miranda when Prospero asked her if she remembered anything of her infancy:

> Of any thing the image tell me, that
> Hath kept with thy remembrance.

She answers:

> 'Tis far off,
> And rather like a dream than an assurance
> That my remembrance warrants. Had I not
> Four or five women once that tended me?

And he again,

> Thou hadst, and more, Miranda. But how is it
> That this lives in thy mind? What seest thou else
> In the dark backward and abysm of time?

The figures coming forward — sometimes at our call, sometimes,
it would seem, by some will we do not identify — may represent
closely or at a far remove persons and things we have known in
life. And as Dryden will also say, this is the same process in
poetry:
"Wit in the poet, or wit writing is the faculty of imagination in
the writer, which, like a nimble spaniel, beats over and ranges
through the field of memory, till it springs the quarry it hunted
after; or, without metaphor, which searches over all the memory
for the species or ideas of those things which it designs to
represent."[20]
Prospero's word "abysm" brings with it the notion of space, a
notion we evidently depend on in our efforts to form conceptions
of time itself — which we must always speak of as near or far,
close at hand or remote. In this evidently inescapable association,
when we think of the abysm, the vasty deep Glendower named —

> I can call spirits from the vasty deep;

only to receive Hotspur's affront —

> But will they come when you do call for them? —

we think of it as the residence of time past and passing. The figuring and sense is thereby accompanied by the notion that all that exists has its origin in place as well as in time. We may go so far as to believe that space works through the instrumentality of time to bring into being whatever is, in reality as it does in thought. In such as association, like Hugo, we are conceiving of an all-bearing source.

Plato went on from just such perceptions to his own marvelous inference. He distinguished between the idea of space accompanying our sense of reality — "everlasting, admitting no destruction, but offering a place for all things that come into being, itself apprehensible without sensation by a sort of bastard reasoning" — and the sense we have when we are dreaming, led at such times to accept images as real in granting them space to occupy, "without which we could not credit them at all." (*Timaeus,* 52 B-D)[21]

He was concluding that the world we do "in fact" inhabit is as uncertainly to be credited as the world of dreams; is to be best spoken of as a strange half-world where we reason as best we can about reality — quite imperfectly — and yet we are bound to depend on our reasoning as much as we do: "It is a dubious kind of existence that is in space; for did not space exist, nothing would remain but the idea; and since the image cannot be in that, it could not be at all."

The ways in which the memory feeds the imagination, providing the sense of place with which to confer "existence" upon what it harbors, are, it seems, the ways in which coming-into-being itself occurs — as the phrase goes, "takes place." And in the knowledge of what is common to both we are led to take as seriously as we do not only what memory provides us with from the urgings of our senses but quite as marvelously from the orderings that have found their way into language over the centuries, and from the incitements of all the arts.

Taking such concerns and delights seriously we call reason into play and draw inferences. As the words of stories, for example, give rise to images, those images may become increasingly distinct and allied to innumerable others. Outlines become figures in two, then in three dimensions, become shaded and colored and dense. As they take on substance and are endowed with motion they come to represent such embodiments of passions and ideas

46

as we acknowledge in those around us. Taking form out of the formless dark they take on such activity as persons in life and as the sense of the space they occupy makes them seem authentic, so in their vividness they cause that space to be all but indistinguishable from the space in which we ourselves live and move.

Enchanted with such accounts — of Orestes, Ulysses, Lady Macbeth — through words and all other representations, as well as in noticing persons in life and hearing their stories, we understand that we are becoming endowed with the knowledge that in due course will substantiate commitments, which in the end is what engages us most profoundly of all. And in retrospect we shall probably be hard put to say which has counted for the most, the encounters with actuality or what has come to us through fictions and the recordings of history.

As a conceit, the notion of the mind as a place also justifies faith in the power thought possesses of appearing to explore — to acknowledge and then to pierce limits. Paradoxically, the idea of the mind's place leads into the sense of limits infinitely extended and of the mind exerting its powers there unceasingly, even conceiving as we are now able to do of universe after universe, and mystically as well, as with Herbert's "Church-bells beyond the stars heard."[22] Paradoxically, too, the notion of the mind's place causes us to conceive of the mind as that which invites occupation, even if in this instance this would be by what is insubstantial — images and motion and some organizing agency accommodating the stirrings in the mind to what our nature as well as reason proposes as salutary or destructive, good or evil. We conceive of this activity of motion and image and thought as an arena, a stage, the playing-area of our conscious as well as our unconscious concerns, in which judgment both openly and covertly discovers the order in the playing.

What we attend to in the images works of art provoke is partly of our own provision and partly of the artists'. Partly determining their effects are not only the immediate utterances and formings but their history as well, the long processes serving the interests of celebration that have validated the languages and the conventions, the vocabularies with which generations have sustained their understanding and their convictions and enjoyments. These bequeathings define the limits as they provide the resources for what the individual day in and day out makes of the passing of time. We are as intent upon the medium that gives resonance to what the words tell of, as intent upon the sense of sounds responding from the deep as upon what the words say — such a sense as Ariel telling of the sounds the nymphs made beneath the sea announcing the death and transformed life of Ferdinand's father:

Full fathom five thy father lies,
Of his bones are coral made,
Those are pearls that were his eyes,
Nothing of him that doth fade
But doth suffer a sea-change
Into something rich and strange;
Sea-nymphs hourly ring his knell:
                    Ding dong.
Hark, now I hear them, ding-dong bell.

Conscious always of our still very different selves we are yet so close to what Ariel is saying, and Homer and all the others, that we might be communing, and while we are certain that this Ariel who so holds us is not our invention but is risen out of the ocean Shakespeare is, we have no doubt that in sounding his depths we are sounding ours. To the sound of hidden bells, out of the stuff of darkness and life, come the marvellous beings we know in discovering ourselves.

The receptacle each of us offers, dark or barely lit, as our attention becomes fixed grows into light, and the figures in our thought become endowed with the dimensions light reveals. We say "we see" to mean "we understand," and again the analogy with Plato is invaluable. It is the sense of the mind as its own place that gives us the confidence to take responsibly the matter entertained there in just that way in which the divine intelligence is said to attest to the reality whose figurings space makes possible — the place that is uniquely our own and that from the beginning already contains whatever the outside world presents to us, the mind itself already instructed to honor what appears to it as existant. And this "place," occupied by this endlessly rich life, provokes the sounds and meanings that lead into language, our own and the race's, that from the beginning foreshadows whatever the outside world brings to us, our minds already instructed to harbor what it acknowledges as real.

All the while I picture and follow Ulysses I am taken quite as much with the strangenesses as with what I observe of myself in all that is taking place; in that continuous noticing of the strange and unfamiliar I am referring one to the other — how what I know in myself could be as this other, and what is so unlike me in him might yet be what I could become. And as my thoughts become increasingly engaged, so do these references become more wide-ranging and deeper; there seems to be no limit to their extension so that I come to feel satisfied — the thoughts that have noticed and fed upon the differences end in convincing me that Ulysses and I — and for that matter, Emaus and Penelope and the others in the story — are but one of my worlds, they are but one of the worlds I possess and exploit.

We do not at our best mistake the illusions works of art incite for other than indices to thought and enjoyment, yet we use them for their worth in offering semblances to what engages our responsibilities. They offer the special advantage of focussing a multitude of considerations upon specific sequences in the actions and states they represent, and in focusing attention they facilitate the judgments we are led to make as if we were treating with occurrences in life. In holding our attention, bringing before us the circumstances of beings resembling those we know, they lead us to reflect upon the decisions we would need to make in like circumstances. In holding us they allow us through fictions, images, even such evocations of the mysterious as hold us in dreams, to discover how we in fact make our own alliances in the world of decision and action. When we follow all Ulysses does, all he must undertake if he is to see his wife and son, we are all the while measuring our concurrence with these requirements — fidelity, truthfulness, enterprise, the compulsions of affection. The imagination permits us to conceive of Ulysses' actions in perfect generosity, blinded neither by stupidity, or envy, and by the trustworthiness of such a gauge we come to know how much or how little scope we ourselves have in the world of actuality. We value the illusions as the means of determining the powers we believe in that are indeed real, and the special quality the greatest imaginative works have for us, distinguished from all others, is in appearing to us in an immaculate light.

V

"For if truth is only sensation, Theataetus, and no man can discern another's feelings better than himself, or has any better right to determine whether his opinion is true or false, but each one is himself the sole judge, and everything that he judges is true and right, why should Protagoras be preferred to the place of wisdom and instruction, and deserve to be well paid, and we poor ignoramuses have to go to him, if each one is the measure of his own wisdom?" (*Theataetus,* 161E)

The scepticism of the *Theataetus* was more than matched centuries afterwards as the reasoning of Descartes made its power felt and as in time classical metaphysics was savaged. The idea of man itself became unmanageable and the notion of the perceiving-and-judging-self was reduced to a phantasm. Where once Protagoras could propose man as the measure of all things, the reasoning of Hume showed that he could have no sure knowledge at all, neither of himself or of his good. Later still, doubt in the ascendant, expanding into positions prepared by further analysis and reduction, advanced the rejection of any of the traditional claims to the knowledge of meaning in human existence. However proposed, whether in a child's imaginings or an adult's speculation's or in the treating of any of the arts with thought, such affirmations were to be interpreted as the body's vaporings or as the projections of minds lost in their own inventions. The race was to be left without a touchstone on the matters that most attract our care, deprived even of such confidence as Protagoras had in his authority. Deprived of stable reference thought and imagining were equally unmoored, and, in particular, the assurance of communication that sustains our delight in words and in responding to them was said to be intoxication.

In speaking of poetry as more philosophical than history Aristotle was remarking that in the attention it pays to particular matters it holds us more powerfully than philosophy, which rests too much with generalities. I believe it is possible, if we extend the reasoning that underlies this assessment, to validate the assurance we so much depend on and that the Cartesian procedures would disqualify, once more persuaded that the conviction of meaning that the arts of language especially encourage is justified.

We may conclude that the falsifications of fiction in the right hands illuminate more truly what experience tells us than the procedures of unending doubt.

Aristotle in effect was turning Protagoras' argument upon its head, for the sceptic in continuously abstracting from experience and thus appealing to generality after generality, most especially when he does this in the name of science, gains only limited authority over our assent, and in certain matters less authority than poetry — fiction — by the obligation science serves in discrediting the appeal particulars in themselves make to our attention. The sceptic, to pursue the Aristotelean discrimination, is led on by an imageless dream; generalization subdues whatever encourages the dominance of the particular in an image, and thereby excludes many of the references sentience is offering to the scrutiny of reason. In the extreme, with Hume and so many following him, we become so distrustful of sense and common sense that we may be persuaded to abandon the idea of a sensing agent as an entity of any kind. If our analysis is rigorous enough we may turn to some notion of "inter-subjectivity," or to some disembodied or transcendent agency thinking through us — the de-centered-self of the structuralists; or, as it has been said of Sartre, to the supposition of "an impersonal stream of consciousness without an 'I.'"[23] The refusal to credit the reality of continuing identities and of the objects of sense and the images they elicit is sustained by the appeal doubt makes in the name of analysis pursued indeflectibly as the warrant of rational and logical integrity.

When we balk at such unpalatable however resistless conclusions we find ourselves in need of arguments that will not only free us from the absurdity of claiming for ourselves the status of non-entity, but that in displacing scepticism will provide reasoning comprehensive enough to accommodate the interests of science as well as fiction. We shall, in short, be led to counter the purest scepticism by observing its own dependence upon faith. But even before then we need to understand something of the grounds for which we respect what poetry offers.

The approximations of fiction bring with them the conviction of valid references, references of "great constancy," where we often discover meanings particularity and generalization both miss. Even inchoate dreams may gain such trust as the event justifies. Valéry put it this way: "Our entire language is made up of brief dreams, and what is so pleasing about this is that we are sometimes able to make thoughts of them that are marvellously exact and at the same time reasonable."[24] The fictions of scepticism may be similarly rewarding but, by their own insistence, only if they can free themselves of the constraints of language, of "dreams"; or, at least, if in their conclusions sceptics should acknowledge the direction they take from their own "dreams," however inchoate. Should this be unacknowledged — as for example, in Hume's reliance upon the image of a flux, or in Lévi-Strauss's continuous recourse to the idea of space giving dimension to mind[25] — they deprive themselves of the finally validating foundation for their thought, such validation as only an image can supply — I believe this means, reliance upon metaphysics. To put it another way, the procedures of doubt pursued inexorably can only be sustained by faith in what is not submitted to doubt.[26]

To say that we use our imaginations in forming conceptions of ourselves, that like children we play with illusion as the means to knowledge, is, it would seem, to cast doubt upon any idea that it is knowledge we are obtaining, least of all knowledge of ourselves. And yet more convincedly than with Descartes in his pronouncement, in holding to our assurance, to the conviction of our power to discriminate between the true and false, assurance becomes doubly sure, and never more firmly than in listening to its categorical denial. The suggestion that life is a dream, that the sense of a continuing identity is illusion, that the notion of a touchstone in reality is without any conceivable support in reason, comes up against Pindar's paradox and is then discarded:

> "Man's life is but a day. What is he? What is he not? He is but a specter of a dream, but when the god-given rays of the sun shine upon him his life becomes radiant." (*Pythian,* VIII, 94-7)

In short, the crux in reasoning that is to be resolved in the defense of the authority of the humanities, and in particular of the claims of fiction and poetry to communicate meaning, centers on how we may credit what is called the self, the human's continuing identity.

Over the centuries the Delphic oracle's injunction, "Know thyself," continues to be heard, understood to signify that self-knowledge is the first and foremost obligation of humans. Gabriel Marcel has referred to this as the "foundation" of philosophy from Plato to Descartes and Hegel. In literature we see something of the extent of its appeal in Petrarch and all that followed from his example in the poetry and thought of Europe: "You will recognize your own thoughts in my words, and I shall appear to have attained the ultimate goal of all eloquence — to have moved the mind of the listener according to my wish, and that with no trouble. It is a sore task for the pleader when he is bent on dragging over to his own view a mind that resists persuasion; but what trouble is there for an argument when it enters the ears of a person whose own thought chimes with what he hears and who, having the evidence of his own experience, in order to yield his assent, requires neither concrete examples, nor weighty authority, nor pointed reasoning, but in silence says to himself, 'It is true.'"[27] The explicit undertaking to sound the depths of this belief by theology was as fruitful.[28]

The oracle proposes an undertaking of limitless duration as a duty. It is a challenge pregnant with the richest of promises — the confirmation of worth; the certifying of purpose; illumination; and composure. One of the chief interpretations antiquity itself insisted on was that humans should know their limitations, which is to say, should know themselves for something less than gods, since through over-weening, in thought as in act, we must forever find our ambitions mocking us. There has always been more than enough testimony to justify that warning for it was clear that no one was a match for long for the forces in nature and the universe, for fate and for fortune. The stories of Prometheus and Oedipus and of Ulysses' disappearance beyond the pillars of Hercules pointed to what all experience corroborated. Nowadays, of course, technology has made so much possible that there are learned men who say flatly that humans now have the power to make over the world. In the words of one of these: "I think we must conclude that man's place in the physical universe is to be its master or at least to be the master of the part he inhabits. It is his place, by controlling the natural forces with his intelligence, to put them to work to his purposes and to build a future world in his own image."[29] Yet the impudence in the phrase — "in his own image" — to say nothing of "It is his place" — should have been enough to reveal the nature of the disappointment in store for us in such a triumph for even in our individual lives humans continue to manifest such weakness and confusion and emptiness even while aspiring to greatness that the ancient admonition would soon enough show its force.

"Countless mistakings hover in men's thoughts,
and there is no way of knowing what it is best
to set our hearts on, now or at the end."
(*Olympian* VII, 25-6)

But it is not only the senses of the oracle we should continue to revere, it is the oracle itself — the one who offers the instruction, the power that has given the words their authoritative influence. In antiquity there was little likelihood that the injunction would be divorced from the story of its provenance, the temple at Delphi and the rites performed there for the god Apollo. The fantasy in Shakespeare of what it must have been like to be present at the rites is the reminder of the inevitable astonishment:

The climate's delicate, the air most sweet;
Fertile the isle, the temple much surpassing
The common praise it bears. . . .
        I shall report,
For most it caught me, the celestial habits
(Me thinks I so should term them) and the reverence
Of the grave wearers. O, the sacrifice!
How ceremonious, solemn, and unearthly
It was i' th' offering! . . .
        But of all, the burst
And the ear-deafening voice of th' oracle,
Kin to Jove's thunder, so surprised my sense
That I was nothing.

And so, as with any moving revelation, even as the need for scrutiny asserts itself, the mystery attached to revelation is acknowledged to be the end as well as the substance of reflection, it is the awe of the revelation itself that incites the inquiry, and in the end remains the overriding wonder.

One of the most powerful sources of the philosophic exposition of the meaning of the Delphic Oracle's "Know thyself" was the Platonic *First Alcibiades*. In his characteristic manner Socrates led Alcibiades to the conclusion he had shown to be necessary if the rulers of a city are to be able to administer justice. They must know themselves, they must learn what governs their own reasoning in determining policy, and how far expediency may be understood to agree with justice — all those matters in short in which reason and the love of justice and the love of the city work together. The ruler must come to know what it is in himself that leads him to the knowledge of what is best, always, most perfect and constant — what is, in short, divine. "And if the soul, my dear Alcibiades, is ever to know herself, must she not look at the soul; and especially at that part of the soul in which her virtue resides, and to another which is like to this? And do we know of any part of our souls more divine than that which has to do with wisdom and knowledge? Then this is that part of the soul which resembles the divine; and he who looks at this and at the whole class of things divine, will be most likely to know himself? And self-knowledge we agree to be wisdom?" (132)

That "looking at the most divine part that is the soul" has been long in preparation — Alcibiades himself, as Socrates put it, had had no preparation, being brought up as most Athenian youths by old servants "fit for nothing." The Persians, it suited him to say, went about it differently, knowing how finely administered growth needed to be if one destined to rule was to rule well. "When the boy reaches fourteen years he is taken over by the royal tutors, as they call them there; these are four men chosen as the most highly esteemed among the Persians of mature age, namely, the wisest one, the justest one, the most temperate, and the bravest. The first teaches him the Magian lore of Zoroastes, son of Horomazes, and that is the worship of the gods; he teaches him to be truthful all his life long; the most temperate, not to be mastered by even a single pleasure, in order that he may be accustomed to be a free man and a veritable king, who is the master of all that is in him, not the slave; while the bravest trains him to be fearless and undaunted, telling him that to be daunted is to be enslaved."

Now, grown up, Alcibiades must learn from such inquiring as Socrates leads him to, "by the mere force of genius alone," what in his being requires him to honor truth, to be temperate, to cultivate wisdom, to be fearless. What would have been instilled had he been brought up by hand he must discover through such patient insistence as reason and discourse would reveal as his

55

proper disposition. He will need all the help he can get. Socrates goes on: "We must put our heads together, you know, as to the way in which we can improve ourselves to the utmost. For observe that when I speak of the need to be educated I am not referring only to you, apart from myself; since my case is identical with yours except in one point."

"What is that?"

"My guardian is better and wiser than yours was — Pericles."

"Who is he, Socrates?"

"God, Alcibiades." (124C)

He has come around to what it has all been about — within himself each human finds what can lead him to the knowledge of wisdom and justice and temperance and courage, these attributes of divinity that divinity alone makes truly known.

Paraphrasing Socrates' reference to divinity, we take him to be referring to a power not so limited as any within the possession of humans. That power is imparted to us when we recognize ourselves in others, and in such speech as soul to soul affordeth, it takes us with delight as we perceive in others the ways we have known life to take with us. This is where the word "divine" becomes apt — for nothing of our own willing or doing could provide a bridge to the strangeness of others, only a power acting upon us, something that might be thought of as possession were it not that the sense of union is effected as much through understanding as in delight.

Attracted as we are by the speculations of antiquity we need to be on guard against accepting imprudently so many of the phrases that have become traditional in literary and philosophic discussions since it appears they are so important to us. When we hear Cassirer taking over the Delphic "Know thyself" to identify "the" crisis in modern thought, and Husserl approving the sense Augustine gave the injunction, we know we are obliged to discover what it is that persists so. And if the subjects are indeed common, if over the centuries there is something close to a common understanding in the efforts to honor this enterprise, then we must believe the centuries have credited a sense to the injunction that differing philosophies have treated but partially. It is neither as idealist or realist or phenemonologist that we respond to Plato's appeal to "the inner man," or to Milton's "Paradise within," or Descartes' *cogito*.

With Socrates as with everyone the terms shift — to speak of the knowledge of the self leads into meanings where the words for soul, person, mind are inter-changed, and where, consequently, one might think, the proper discriminations are lost. The difficulty is in the complexity of the conception of individual identity, yet there are many times when Socrates, for example, is as rigorous as anyone can be in refining the senses he gives the words. The word "soul" (psyche) is pretty surely a name given the self in signifying the self as the object of knowledge (*Laches* 185E).[30] This conception leads in a thoroughly responsible way, in the *Charmides,* into the development of the argument that self-knowledge is the virtue temperance itself. As a virtue it is a power, as knowing is a power, in this instance manifested in the exercise of those elements of the person employed in serving the person's good. The magnificent affirmation from the *Meno* is always to be brought to bear: "That we shall be better and braver and less helpless if we think that we ought to inquire than we should have been if we indulged in the idle fancy that there was no knowing and no use in seeking to know what we do not know; — that is a theme upon which I am ready to fight, in word and deed, to the utmost of my power." (86)

And with the same breath we may be led to speak with the *Phaedrus:* "Perhaps I cannot know myself, perhaps I am a beast more strangely wild and more fiery with pride than Typhon." (229E)

When we undertake to follow what Socrates had in mind in describing the process by which he inquires into this "knowledge" we notice the obvious, that each question in finding an answer finds one that leads to another question, and there is also the as important point, the confidence that inspired the questioning is apparently justified, the answers that are found do provide proper foundations for further questioning. In this substantiation of the belief in the worth of the inquiry we observe the remarkable phenomenon that in gross terms is spoken of as the identification of the knower with the known, in which the appeal is made by analogy with the union of the lover with what is loved. The Platonic philosophy presses this conclusion into the most complex ramifications for in the end there will be the conclusion that the knowledge of the self, having truth for its object, becomes the knowledge of truth itself. The advances in the inquiry — swift or halting, wholly or only partly — are understood to be advances not only in the acquisition of truths, but into the knowledge of the basis of being.

If it is right to think of the universe of consciousness and the world without to be in correspondence, it could follow that the knowledge of the self would provide acquaintance with the principles of the great world as well. With Plato it is said to go like this: ". . . the universe is such that the kind of action possible in it is the kind of action which can be productive of inner wholeness. Plato's aim is toward bringing the internal justice or wholeness into unity with external justice, or the harmony, of the whole universe."[31] Many modern materialists and determinists speak of like integrations; in the Platonists, however, the stress upon the personal is decisive — Alcibiades, learning of his own nature, becomes the more perfectly that self he learns of in another; in the end he becomes acquainted with the process through which he and all else participate in the realm of being.

In later developments, as in Plotinus, the soul is said to know itself only in the degree that it is illuminated by the divine reason itself which vouchsafes its light for the soul to see by. And in the entire tradition there is inherent the conclusion Augustine made everything of: "It is in the inner man that you renew yourself, in the image of God; know, then, God in His image." (*In Joan.* 17, 10)

But that step from turning inward — "the inner man" is Plato's phrase as well (*Republic* 589a) — to the discovery of the likeness of the human to the divine order, is not simply effected. The examination of the self proceeds by discourse, and whereas in the beginning there may be an imagined partner — in circumstances not unlike Sidney's —

Fool, said my Muse to me, look in thy heart and write!
— by virtue of the dependence upon language, if for no other reason — an instrument with which each one's people has endowed him — each will need to speak with others in order to pursue the inquiry: with Alcibiades; with the boy in the *Meno* who knew all sorts of proportions without knowing that he did; with the psychiatrist.

And so we return to our question — what means do we have when we refer to the Delphic Oracle that is both fair to traditional senses and valid in the light of so much that we subscribe to since

Descartes? — in general, to all that exercises us in our efforts to assess the claims of objectivity and the falsifications of subjectivity? What in the climate of the modern age are we to regard as well-being that will accord with the older definitions of the powers and limitations of humans? What right have we to use the word "inner," and to speak of an "inner life"? How may we refer responsibly to the idea of personal identity in words that depend so intimately on their affiliations with ancient ways of thought that they appear to put aside the refinements and modifications and refusals that the history of thought has since given rise to?

Acknowledging all such questioning we appeal at the beginning and perhaps at the end as well to common experience and to the authority of common speech, however much these fly in the face of current analytical dispositions. For one thing, we are quite at home with the idea of the certainty of our being, of our character, of patterns in our dispositions and appetites and ways of reasoning, and we demand that our confidence be respected — as Gilson put it, it is absurd to deny what the experience of every day confirms. We are quite accustomed to the idea of remaining the same while the days pass. We are quite agreeable to acknowledge the reality of the habit of a tree, all that congeries of powers and matter that directs the elm tree in its growth to continue in the form of an elm. Only in reasoning of ourselves, in this recognition of our submission to law and form, we include the sense of watching over our passage through time, the consciousness of what our being is making of time and change, and together with all this there is the conviction that by choice, within limits, in flourishing and decay we assert a certain power over time, over the use our bodies and our spirits make of it, over the habit of our existence, and even over something more, over destiny. We acknowledge, it appears, not only the reality of our freedom but of our power.

We understand, of course, that the self is no measureable, visible entity; nothing, either, of the nature of an abstraction, "thought divorced from a thinker." This self that we honor as both the nurse and child of our imaginings we know to be like Proteus, never to be fixed by definition, never to be circumscribed by thought, yet we never doubt it to be imbued with a single identity, a wonder-working power at once guide and source.[32] Shakespeare's image for constancy in love — "an ever-fixed star" — points to what we appeal to in undertaking to know ourselves. As with that image, we hold to the sense of what is ever to be trusted, of what is beyond reach, of what gives light and guides, of what favors our loves. Like the habit of a tree imposing its form upon the changes wind and sun and rain and life and death bring, it maintains itself serenely, intimate to all our motions.

It is perverse to doubt the obvious yet it is evidently necessary to recognize that in underwriting the convictions of identity and constancy questions form endlessly — what is this time whose successions we anticipate with such passion? What power is there in this idea of the future bearing within itself the forms of our perfection, the present being unending possibility? What is this substance time is forever giving form to? The questions are so various, their urgency so persistent, that even when our efforts are unwavering we may find no other ending than in Socratic ignorance, knowing that we do not know. But then again, as also with Socrates, assured there is something to know.

However unending our uncertainties, in continuing to believe reasoning will make us "less helpless," we inevitably appeal to a power residing in the self as trustworthy as the star Shakespeare names, finding such confirmation also as Pindar does, in the light that suffuses thought and that graces illusion —

"The grace, that makes all things for mortals as sweet as honey, brings honors, and time and again makes us believe things past belief." (*Olympian* I, 30–1)

A child's mind is continuously alive with the notion that he is communicating perfectly with all he addresses and all that he takes to be addressing him. To others what appears to be conviction with him is so far from warranted we may think he is inviting madness even as we acknowledge that he is influencing the form his life will be taking through this disposition he finds so attractive. In the old phrase, he is wiser than he knows. And he is in fact through such endeavors discovering his proper habit. He is learning something of what he is, and more of what he may become.

When he is grown he attends *Aida;* reading, he supposes it is Socrates he is answering in some argument; before a television screen, cheering on the players who do not know he exists, he gives them the most explicit directions with the full love and

60

vehemence of his soul. Quite as fruitfully as for the child, in the sense of perfect communication he is discovering the implications of what he takes to be his good, of what he holds to be the worth of life. What he initiates as attention is resolved in communion. So it seems, and in varying degrees it is. The processes of fear and hope in the Egyptian princess; confusions dissipated as Socrates extends his scrutiny; the ebb and flow of the fortunes of the football team: the pattern in all such matters he recognizes as the stuff of his own consciousness and the object of his care, the substance of the concerns of his nature originally and now of his thought. What he responds to outside himself he knows has found its likeness within. In discovering the ways of the world he recognizes his own. His delight, his sympathy, his participation in the successes and defeats of others, which absorb him because they are those of others, take him out of himself. He all but becomes these others in knowing that sensation and reflection within him are following as rapidly as in the music of the opera, in the dartings of another's thought, in the exchanges of a game. His own consciousness is lightning-swift not only in mirroring but also in anticipating, and this immediacy is all he needs to recognize in order to confirm him in the conviction of shared identity.

He all but becomes lost in these others, other living beings or their fictional creations or their reasonings. That "all but" saves the adult from the delusions that tempt the child. Yet for all that he gives of himself he retains the sense of solitude; for all the passion of his concern his delight is equally in knowing how far he remains untouched by these fictions and suppositions and lies. He depends on his capacity for the impossible, for becoming these others, but he does so, and he knows he does so, in order to come to know himself, something other than his inventing or dreaming. The world is so made that fiction and truth are ever treating with each other, and we, in our imaginings and the play of sympathy, come to such terms as we can with truth.

Those we converse with, or imagine we converse with, possess their own inviolable solitude — we credit them with what we hold to in ourselves. We credit all uniqueness, not abandoning our knowledge and honoring of this even when communication is most satisfactory. We recognize ourselves in others, persons in life or in fiction. The fictions are the shadows of their authors much as we are of our friends, shadows cast by the light of others' minds, sharing something that is invaluable to us in coming to know ourselves, and yet not all. Socrates explained to Alcibiades that as the eye, in order to see itself, looks into another eye, so that soul that is to know itself must look upon another soul. Socrates is doing what we all do when we say "I see" to mean "I understand." We are likening sight to thought, and when we speak of looking upon another soul, recognizing the existence of that other, we are seeing, apprehending with our thought, our own thought in that other. Such is the accrual of wisdom, *sophia*. (*Alcibiades* I, 133). And so Shakespeare:

> nor doth the eye itself,
> That most pure spirit of sense, behold itself,
> Not going from itself, but eye to eye opposed,
> Salutes each other with each other's form.
>
> (*Troilus and Cressida,* III, iii, 105-8)

What he sees in himself he sees by the light cast by others' thoughts. He depends on these to know himself, not only through their thoughts but through the power they have to take him into their consideration as he is including them. It may be right to do as Socrates does, to speak of the soul as looking at another soul, and as that which is most divine in the soul, that which is the seat of knowledge and thought, wisdom, hereby coming "to know all that is divine, who shall gain thereby the most assured knowledge of himself." It may be well enough to take Shakespeare's words with their outmoded physiological psychology to tell of that state in which we believe we know ourselves in exchanging glances. Just as every impulse that is a picturing depends on acknowledging other worlds than those within us, so our utterances discover words and orderings for them, embodiments of the motives of our living, just as we suppose ourselves to be embodied, our uniqueness. What we see in exchanging glances we are moved to explore and expound in uttering words and in exchanging them.

And then we discover that even our momentary delights are foreshadowed in the language we are learning, our very destinies have been foreseen, being part and parcel of the history of our peoples. Saint Paul extended the old figure of the world's body into the sense of the mystical union of the baptized with the body of Christ, and in searching out the words and in ordering words, discovering them to be already at hand, we learn as very likely we could not otherwise not merely what we come to know in knowing another, but what we must recognize as what we have in common with other persons.

The oracle's injunction remains in force by virtue of our belief in the autonomy of the individual, a belief most surely evident in the effort deliberately undertaken to obtain self-knowledge. And in addition, it remains in force because in searching the mystery we are holding to the sense of the sacred.

VI

The gains in understanding that have followed upon "desacralization," "depersonalization," "dehumanization," of nature and of humans, have led to the exercise of power over nature, humans, and matter. Power has invited use, and there are few who have not felt drawn, or even obliged, to exercise it in a multitude of possible and practicable ways. The specially qualified pursue the enterprise indefatigably and with the support of scientific organization, the rest of us intermittently however much the charm of mechanics permeates our thinking.

If the enterprises of technology were undertaken automatically, as reflex actions so to speak, there would be little reason to comment upon them as the results of attraction or obligation but this is not the case. They present themselves as opportunities that invite mastery, a demand we respond to as inherent in the opportunities — as such self-perpetuating since they support the capacities that involved us initially in the enterprise.

The advantages are increasingly within the grasp of more and more persons. The instrument seems at hand for enhancing the prosperity of the race and for prolonging indefinitely the lives of individuals. To many, accordingly, the use of power to these ends becomes an obligation, the preeminent one, power now superseding the quest for understanding, there appearing to be no reason to question the desirability of survival in the terms the new measures set, survival defined as continuing the exercise of power.

Any number of sophisticated expressions are on record to this effect and I quote again the director of the Institute for Geo-Physical Research at an American university:

"I think we must conclude that man's place in the physical universe is to be its master or at least the master of the part that he inhabits. It is his place, by controlling the natural forces with his intelligence, to put them to work to his purposes and to build a future world in his image."

It is noteworthy that a rhetorician forwards the same proposition — one other indication of the extent to which the humanities have assimilated a scientistic mentality:

". . . In the present state of human affairs, having become Promethean, man must make supreme efforts to be his own maker and guardian by taking full charge of his institutions and of himself. It is indispensable and unpostponable for man to revise radically the very foundations of his individual and social existence — even what has been sacred and holy for him — to surmount his actual being in order to realize his authentic possibilities, and to create conditions around himself and within himself which will give him a reasonable chance of continued existence on the earth. . . . A theory of argumentation refined with the process of rendering good reasons for our thought and action has thus the highest priority today."[33]

Paradoxically through the means of the very instrument — sceptical analysis — that has dissipated confidence in the existence of the self — there is established a stunning confidence in the power within the compass of the self — over matter and nature and "the universe." The self, as an identity, may not be consulted, although its powers, conceived of as "impersonal," lead to what is obviously, that is to say verifiably, control over the meaningless stuff analysis works upon. It is confusing, however irresistible, to conceive of the results of the use of that power as an imposition of the human "image" upon the universe, which I take to mean, what many do mean, that the universe is what humans wish to make of it. According to the reasoning that disallows inherent worth in anything humans have no special right to domination, but the means being ours it is apparently imperative to employ them.

Yet our successes do point to factors that threaten the continuance of the entire enterprise. The accretions of knowledge and power in one pursuit may lead to results that hinder advance in another. The successes in prolonging life may conflict with the interest leading to the proliferation of life through new means, and both these undertakings may be ruined by the direct as well as the side-effects of the exploitation of energy. Scientists and technologists are progressing within their own areas, in general without coordinating direction. The issue is not merely political, it inheres in the prevailing view of the nature of science. Were study pursued in the light of an interest relating parts to wholes, in some such way as those studies that look to the preservation of "the balance of nature," conflict and anarchy would not be the necessary outcome. This is what Werner Heisenberg has in mind: "What is really needed is a change in fundamental concepts. We will have to abandon the philosophy of Democritus and the concept of fundamental elementary particles. And, instead, we will have to accept the concept of fundamental symmetries which is a concept out of the philosophy of Plato.

"Just as Copernicus and Galileo abandoned in their method the descriptive science of Aristotle and turned to the structural science of Plato, so we are probably being forced in our concepts to abandon the atomic materialism of Democritus and to turn to the ideas of symmetry in the philosophy of Plato."[34] Deprived of any such cosmological orientation as the *Timaeus* develops, scientists and technologists must be prepared to have the state limit their works.

The question returns — What is "the proper study," its methods and its object? Professor Libby is right about this, science is disposed to regard human beings and their activities as intelligible in the same terms assigned to material configurations. Put the same thought in different words, however, and it becomes a matter for dismay rather than for exultation: "Hereafter all further progress in science, whether in abstract speculation or practical application — and the two are inseparable — can only emphasize depersonalization, this submission to a perspective that transforms man into an object."[35] But this "object" is an indefatigable inquirer and power seeker and tyrant — object over and against object. At this point one may put aside the metaphor of the universe as "the image" of man to return to the more common similitude, a mechanism involved in the infinite meshings of other mechanisms, motors of the same nature working through all. It may be that consciousness distinguishes humans but this so far may not be proposed as altering the nature of the mechanical operations. Yet consciousness makes special demands upon our notice, it will not keep silent, it keeps reminding us that so far the effort to define it as quantifiable, voiceless energy has failed. On the other hand it offers little enough to lead the reasoning another way, and is indeed enough of an accomplice to the mechanists to be anxious to share the credit for this indefatigable labor subduing the outer world. And by the very fact that it provides a voice, an expression from outside as it were, a recording but also a critical apparatus, we take it at its word, as do Professor Libby and Professor Tammelo. It speaks as if it were freely authorizing the conquests of the disembodied self. Being so plainly a boast we are invited to subject it to the scrutiny we give any boast, finding a disconcerting discrepancy in consciousness identifying itself with an "object."

In our assessment of this being that takes upon itself the responsibility for rescuing us from own limitless subjection (to what is not clear), we notice that the boast is being made by a being not at the moment engaged in the scientific enterprise, it speaks — to parody an earlier comment — "in the optative mode." And this leads us into another view of the matter.

Pascal pursued his perception of the infinite into the "abyss" within the atom: "Let man see therein an infinity of universes, each of which has its firmament, its planets, its earth, in the same proportions as in the visible world; in each earth animals, and in the last mites, on which he will find again all that the first had, finding still in these others the same thing without end and without cessation." Nothing that could be said now could say more — a speck within a speck, vaunting itself.

And then we notice another feature of this Titanic character — like the universe he takes over he is perfectly manageable, wholly predictable, perpetually in motion, perfectly self-serving, perpetually victorious even over death, at least if ignoring it is to be thought a victory.

A remarkable irony is now apparent — although immense power is within reach and limitless power aspired to, the individual indispensable to the enterprise is not to be valued as an individual. Engaged in a search which is by definition endless, dependent on most complexly articulated cooperation with other individuals, he knows as never before that sense of isolation in which Hume found himself in blessing the reasoning that would sustain these remarkable advances. Hume had the advantage of his wonderful intelligence in comprehending the state at which he had arrived, while most of those enlisted in following the ways of scepticism and analysis may be nearly blind. Having learned that it is "man," not "men," who are charged to carry on, each one, alone, ignored, as for a while the Ancient Mariner feared he was, is asked to be content to be a number. The knowledge of being cast upon this barren vastness counters and in the end may poison the joy of mastery. Even the joy he takes in exulting over those he has discountenanced — the Aristoteleans, the vitalists, the religious — becomes arid when he is reminded that what he cares for as a person is of no value, that the very idea of solace as of the sweetness of companionship has been invalidated. The sceptical reasoning that laid the foundations for such astounding successes, enabling these nameless individuals to do for all humans what those displaced could never have done — keeps telling him he is a nonentity — a "consciousness without an I," "a de-centered self." And yet such power is now within the possession of these innumerable — what Dante might call — shades, that each asks himself to become Prometheus. And so the idea spreads among the very masses aspiring to such eminence Cola di Rienzo aimed at — Tribune of Rome, Senator, a new Holy Roman Emperor of the Universe. Petrarch's disillusionment is also that of each part of us that cannot reflect upon our isolation except in grief:

"I thought I saw you in a lofty place, at the center of the world, so high you could almost touch the sky. A great crowd of men of courage surrounded you and you stood in the midst of them, on a splendid throne, dominating them all. I asked someone what it all meant, this crowd of men twenty times greater than the population of the entire world. I asked someone what it all could mean, and he told me there were present not only all the men now alive but all who ever would be, all the races of mankind into eternity, and I asked myself what did I think would come of all this, this man at the height of all human power.

"So I spoke to him and I said, think carefully about what you are, analyze yourself carefully, try to remember, without deception, who you are, what you have been, where you came from, how far you may go without compromising your freedom, where

67

you are going, what role you have undertaken, what name you have taken on, what hopes you have awakened, what promises you have made, and you will see that you are not the master of all this, but the slave."

And so we are returned to the question — what is "the proper study?" — man as perfectly controllable as the universe itself is, infinite but wholly predictable, perpetually in motion, Promethean, self-serving; or, a frail, thinking reed; the image of God; the perfection of nature: "the conqueror of all save death"? And taking any or all these images, we may interpret them as Professor Libby does, or in the very terms Professor Libby provides, or as Milton in the words he gave Satan:

(Seeking)
Our own good from ourselves, and from our own
Live to ourselves, though in this vast recess,
Free, and to none accountable, preferring
Hard liberty before the easy yoke
Of servile pomp. Our greatness will appear
Then most conspicuous, when great things of small,
Useful of hurtful, prosperous of adverse
We can create.

The final comment is possibly this: "The means determine the ends, by assigning us ends that can be attained and eliminating those considered unrealistic because our means do not correspond to them. At the same time, the means corrupt the ends. We live at opposite ends of the formula that the ends justify the means. We should understand that our enormous present means shape the ends we pursue. The means of national or class war have become such that just because they exist, we can no longer hope to establish peace; the means of coercion are such that they no longer permit us to claim that thanks to them we will arrive at liberty."[36]

But the fact remains that in the present state of things any image of ourselves that we accept will not return us to a state in which the world in which we think is also the world in which we live — we remain committed to unending discovery, aspiring to rule over all our divided self has presented to us, still cut off from amity and union and the fullness of being we continue to dream of. But the memory of past glories and defeats is not effaced, it continues to assure us of our continuing identity, that we are not the first to aspire to illimitable conquests, and that certitude has never yet come into the possession of humans.

NOTES

[1] *From Hume to the Vienna Circle,* Harmondsworth, n.d., p. 204.

[2] Hans Jonas, *Philosophical Essays,* Englewood Cliffs, 1974, p. 12.

[3] *Personal Knowledge,* Chicago, 1974, p. 173.

[4] *The Laws of Ecclesiastical Polity,* I. ix. 12.

"And the queen of Saba, having heard of the fame of Solomon in the name of the Lord came to try him with hard questions . . . And Solomon informed her of all the things she proposed to him: there was not any word the king was ignorant of, and which he could not answer her . . . And she said to the king: The report is true, which I heard in my own country concerning thy words and concerning thy wisdom. And I did not believe them that told me, till I came myself, and saw with my own eyes, and have found that the half hath not been told me. Thy wisdom and thy works exceed the fame which I heard. Blessed are thy men, and blessed are thy servants, who stand before thee always, and hear thy wisdom." *I Kings,* 10: 1-8.

[5] "L'Existentialisme chez Hegel," in *Sens et Non-Sens,* Paris, 1967, p. 69.

[6] Helmut Kuhn, "Personal Knowledge and the Crisis of the Philosophical Tradition," in *Intellect and Hope,* edd. T.A. Langford and W.H. Poteat, Durham, North Carolina, 1968, p. 120.

[7] "The conclusions that there are telic phenomena is inescapable, but also so incredible to most scientists and to a public nourished in the mythology of purely one-level, purely 'mechanistic' science, that it is suppressed as a piece of lingering superstition or wilful obscurantism. In this century alone, Bergson, Whitehead, Alexander, Collingwood, Husserl, Merleau-Ponty, Polanyi among philosophers; E. S. Russell, J. S. Haldane, Cuenot, Vandel, Spemann, R. S. Lillie, Portmann, Buytendijk, Straus, Goldstein — and a number of others — among biologists have presented irrefutable refutations of a dogmatic mechanism. Yet, over and over, every doubt of current dogma is swept aside as dogmatism. To be sceptical of teleology is 'scientific,' even if this means denying what is as plain as the nose on one's face. To be sceptical of such dogmatic denial, on the other hand, we are constantly told, is to deny altogether the cogency of 'scientific method.' What can lend credit to a truth so implausible in the eyes of most authorities?

"The trouble is that the denial of teleology fits smoothly into the metaphysical 'paradigm' (in Kuhn's sense) of the world machine, while its assertion either hangs, a bare statement, unframed by an adequate cosmology, or, worse still, seems to the proponents of objectivism a revival of the scholastic absurdities which Science had so triumphantly overcome." (Marjorie Grene, *The Knower and the Known,* London, 1966, p. 239.)

[8] Suzanne Lilar, *A Propos de Sartre et de l'Amour,* Paris 1969, p. 69.

[9] Mikel Dufrenne, *Language & Philosophy*, tr. H. B. Veatch, Bloomington, 1963, p. 40.

[10] *A Treatise of Human Nature*, IV, vi.

[11] *Ibid.*, IV. vii.

[12] Gérard Bonnot, *Ils Ont Tué Descartes*, Paris, 1969, p. 216.

[13] Roger W. Sperry, "Mind, Brain and Humanist Values," in *New Views of the Nature of Man*, ed. John R. Platt, Chicago, 1965, p. 75.

[14] Paul Roubouczek, *Ethical Values in the Age of Science*, Cambridge, 1969, p. 86.

[15] Sydney Shoemaker, *Self-Identity and Self-Knowledge*, Ithaca, 1963, p. 258.

[16] "C'est une chose très assurée que personne ne peut être certain s'il pense et s'il existe, si, primièrement, il ne connaît la nature de la pensée et de l'existence. Non que pour cela il soit besoin d'une science réfléchie, ou acquise par une démonstration, et beaucoup moins de la science de cette science, par laquelle il connaisse qu'il sait, et derechef qu'il sait qu'il sait, et ainsi jusqu'à l'infini, étant impossible qu'on en puisse jamais avoir une telle d'aucune chose que ce soit; mais il suffit qu'il sache cela par cette sorte de connaissance intérieure qui précède toujours l'acquise, et qui est si naturelle à tous les hommes, en ce qui regarde la pensée et l'existence, que, bien que peut-être étant aveuglés par quelques pré-jugés, et plus attentifs au son des paroles qu'à leur véritable signification, nous puissions feindre que nous ne l'avons point, il est néanmoins impossible qu'en effet nous ne l'ayons." (*Réponses de l'Auteur aux Sixièmes Objections faites par divers Théologiens, Philosophes et Géomètres*, in *Oeuvres Philosophiques*, ed Ferdinand Alquié, II (Paris, 1967), 861-2.)

[17] *Mémoire et Personne*, Paris, 1951, pp. 420-1.

[18] Fernand Robert, *L'Humanisme*, Paris, 1946, pp. 129-30.

[19] *Science et Humanisme*, Paris, 1947, p. 15.

[20] "*Annus Mirabilis:* An Account of the Ensuing Poem," in *The Poetical Works*, Cambridge, 1909, p. 25.

[21] What Dryden and Hugo bring forward are imaginative conceits, fictions of suggestive power, and although these were no doubt obliged to philosophy they are not offered as other than figures of speech to encourage thought.

When we in a quite different intellectual climate respond to them we bring to bear reasoning from our own times, and we find ourselves validating our responses in appeals to more sophisticated philosophizing. Accordingly, after referring Dryden's and Hugo's images to Plato and Augustine, we find that we refer our own to contemporary ideas of time and space. A comment of Mr. E. E. Harris may help show how our adaptation of the ancient images and terms is nourished by ideas of relativity: "The metaphysical conception engendered by the theory of relativity is one in which the space-time continuum functions as the primordial stuff or substance of the material world. Implicit in the structure of its intrinsic diversification are the existence, physical properties and behavior of material bodies. Space-time is consequently no featureless void but an ordered plenum, in which both the aspect of fullness and that of internal organization have far-reaching philosophical significance." He goes on to distinguish this conception from Plato's. "The relativistic conception of space leads to a position in some ways reminiscent (despite obvious differences) of Plato's account of the 'receptacle' in the *Timaeus* (49-52) . . . But whereas the Platonic 'receptacle' (or 'recipient') has no form of its own and simply receives the forms imposed upon it, Einstein's space-time has an intrinsic structure which regulates the order of events (and so of all spatial relations and movements) within it." (*The Foundations of Metaphysics in Science*, London, 1965, pp. 64 and 68.)

[22] This is much as it was with Bruno: "Time after time, Bruno attacks the conception of space as 'that which encloses,' the soma periekon of Peripatetic physics. For Bruno, the space in which the universe exists is not the farthest boundary in which, so to speak, the universe is embedded and wrapped: rather, space is the free medium of movement, extended unhindered beyond every finite border and in all directions." (Ernst Cassirer, *The Individual and the Cosmos*, New York, 1963, p. 187.)

[23] Samuel Spiegelberg, *The Phenomenological Movement*, The Hague, 1960, p. 480.

[24] *Petite Lettre sur les Mythes*, Paris, 1929, p. 6.

[25] "Ma seppure ricondotto tutto a *système*, l'inconscio di Lévi-Strauss ha comunque una sua consistenza reale. Basterebbe riflettere su tutte le metafore spaziali che il padre dell'antropologia strutturale adopera parlando del tema in questione. L'inconscio, abbiam già letto, è un "piano" che si "raggiunge": dunque è qualcosa che ha un suo spazio, una sua collocazione, e dunque anche una sua consistenza. Questa consistenza è in qualche modo attestata anche dal fatto che in vari scritti teorici (sopratutto degli anni '50) la struttura inconscia viene presentata come il luogo 'abitato' dalle categorie più generali dello spirito. Vi abitano, va rilevato, in modo tutt'altro che metaforico-formale: è lí, è da lí, come sarà detto in qualche pagina particolarmente significativa, che tali categorie esplicano la loro opera plasmante e condizionante. . . ." (Sergio Moravia, *La Ragione Nascosta*, Florence, 2nd ed., 1972, pp. 296-7.)

[26] "Science is a system of beliefs to which we are committed. Such a system cannot be accounted for either from experience as seen within a different system, or by reason without any experience. Yet this does not signify that we are free to take it or leave it, but simply reflects the fact that it *is* a system of beliefs to which we are committed and which therefore cannot be represented in non-committal terms." (Michael Polanyi, *Personal Knowledge*, Chicago, 1974, p. 171.)

[27] *De Vita Solitaria*, tr. Jacob Zeitlin, I. i.

[28] Something of the scope of the subject may be seen in Pierre Courcelle, " 'Nosce Teipsum' du Bas-Empire au Haut Moyen-âge. L'Héritage profane et les développements Chrétiens," in *Il Passaggio dall'Antichità al Medioevo in Occidente*, Spoleto, 1962, pp. 265-95.

[29] W. F. Libby, in *New Views of the Nature of Man*, ed. J. R. Platt, Chicago, 1965, p. 14.

[30] "The identification of the soul with the self is the conclusion of an argument in *Alcibiades* I (127-130), and "This is just the view that Plato represents Socrates as taking at the end of the *Phaedo* (115c-d) . . . The real Socrates . . . is the one at present taking part in discussion with [his friend] and marshalling the various arguments, not the one soon to be seen as a corpse." (Norman Gulley, *The Philosophy of Socrates*, London, 1968, p. 198.)

[31] E. G. Ballard, *Socratic Ignorance*, The Hague, 1965, p. 153.

[32] A psychiatrist has been quoted as saying that the self in looking to know itself finds itself in "a wilderness of mirrors." A more detailed expression of this view is this:

"According to current social-psychological theory, some of the subselves in a single total personality derive more or less directly from the internalization of parental figures, bad ones as well as good ones. Some subselves come from heroes, from rivals as well as friends; some come from fantasy preoccupations; some come from institutional roles — in the school, the church, the army, the office and the shop; and some come from males and some from females. The total personality can be conceptualized as a group of interacting tendencies, each approaching a subself in complication: subselves with different origins, different characters, associations, value implications, behavioral manifestations, and so on. From this set of assumptions it is a problem to understand how the actual individual ever manages to pull himself together, and one is not surprised to detect a lack of complete consistency." (R. F. Bales, *Personality and Interpersonal Behavior,* New York, 1970, p. 15.)

In this way of thinking the awareness of others, in part effected through sight, leads to a condition quite unlike what Socrates tells of. In the Socratic figuring the mind goes forward in the "exchange" as with Donne's "our eye-beams twisted" — to discover not the self's deficiency but the way of its perfection. It is much the same with Aristotle when he says that we know ourselves through the eyes of a friend, for the friend is another self (*Magna Moralia,* 1213).

There are of course even more primitive references to this means of authorizing conviction — E. R. Dodds speaks of the earlier notions as "a personalized *genius loci." (The Greeks and the Irrational,* Berkeley, 1964, pp. 14-15.) There is more of the primitive than the Socratic in the Hegelian conception as Kierkegaard interprets it: "This daimonic lies in the transition from the oracle's external relation to the individual to the full inwardness of freedom, and, as still being in the transition, it pertains to representation." *(The Concept of Irony,* tr. L. M. Capel, New York, 1965, pp. 190-1).

Valéry anticipates the socio-psychological theory (deriving from Descartes) in the *Sixth Meditation* that Merleau-Ponty approved: "No one could think freely if his eyes could not take leave of different eyes which followed them. As soon as glances meet, we are no longer wholly two, and it is hard to remain alone. This exchange (the term is exact) realizes in a very short time a transposition or metathesis — a chiasma of two 'destinies,' two points of view. Thereby a sort of simultaneous reciprocal limitation occurs. You capture my image, my appearance, I capture yours. You are not *me,* since you see me and I do not see myself. What I lack is this me that you see. And what you lake is the you I see. And no matter how far we advance in our mutual understanding, as much as we reflect, so much will we be different." (*Tel Quel,* I. Paris, 1941, pp. 41-2.)

For Valéry the exchange of glances, continued and repeated, leading to some understanding, ends in the more certain sense of "lack," that is to say, not only of ultimate loneness but of deficiency. This follows of necessity by virtue of exclusive reliance upon observation — the detachment of the Cartesian "thing that thinks." Words have not been called upon in the exchange to reveal the soul, as Socrates has it, and certainly not to include reference to the divine logos that is the medium for the communication and ennoblement Socrates says we discover.

As I see it the reasoning of both Bales and Valéry ends in a cul-de-sac because they are ignoring their own use of a constant, the idea of a continuing identity which alone allows for the detection of multiplicity.

[33] Ilmar Tammelo, "The Rule of Law and the Rule of Reason in International Legal Relations," in *La Théorie de l'Argumentation,* Louvain, n.d. (Centre Nationale de Recherches de Logique), p. 367.

[34] *Encounter,* XLIV (3), March, 1975, p. 59.

[35] Gérard Bonnot, *Ils On Tué Descartes,* Paris, 1969, p. 247.

[36] Jacques Ellul, *The Political Illusion,* tr. Konrad Kellen, New York, 1967.

The Proper Study

The worth of many undertakings in the social sciences is incontestable. One has only to remind oneself of studies of primitive peoples, how these have enriched our notions of the range and variety of human experience, how they have instructed us in making discriminations we might not have been prepared for in the examination of theirs and of our own communities. Herodotus and Marco Polo of course preceded Sir James Frazier, and Malinowski and Lorenz no doubt have brought to their studies the advantages of certain methods and means of measurement those earlier inquirers could not employ, but all alike have shown us the uses of comparison. And if what these and others have brought forth has not persuaded us that even an exhaustive survey of the peoples of the earth would provide the final determination of the range of human capacities, they have certainly led us to refine and to continue to try to refine our understanding of all that is involved in biology and morality.

The old phrase, "Nothing human is alien to me," embodies many ideas and convictions, and among them this most specially, that self-knowledge, some meaningful although ultimately mysterious exploration of an individual's consciousness, sets the terms for any study of others that aspires to verification. The ancient assertion rests upon a faith that we find grows stronger with the accretions of experience. In the progressions of feelings and thoughts we become confirmed as we look at those about us in the conviction that they are persons as we are persons. In the presence of those to whom I attribute humanity I recognize myself. If, when I imagine myself joining with Othello in his adventures, I do not see everything exactly as he does, if I do not

75

respond in quite the same way in the encounter with the Anthropophagi, and those who bear their heads beneath their shoulders, yet I believe I share something of the same shock, I feel I am met with some such lack of recognition as he too, must have felt, and even believe that I was stirred as he was with something of the like fellow-feeling.

But there are meanings in the phrase of Terence that the anthropologist, for example, might find misleading or distracting. If, for example, I should be accompanying Othello not as a companion in arms or a sutler but as a scientist, no doubt I should resist the allurements of Terence's conclusions for as a scientist I would hold fast to the obligation to entertain the possibility of the wholly alien at the very instant I should be recognizing the familiar. I must be prepared to discover not only among monsters but among humans something I had not known of, even what I may never know, about them or about myself. I must be prepared to explore what I had thought to be beyond the limits of the human, even to discover the inhuman. I may discover rather definite distinctions — among peoples who tolerate extremely low temperatures, or who have developed remarkable faculties in testing the uses of herbs, and I may so far pass beyond the range of experience I had previously supposed to set limits upon the human that I find I must range among and study beasts. Or as we sometimes say horribly of some afflicted persons, among those who have become vegetables.

I speculate that, as a scientist, I may be able to pass beyond the threshold certain ancient Christians respected when they refused to baptize those whom in the supposed absence of humanity they called dogs. Not otherwise, probably, than the Greeks who excluded the barbarians. As a scientist I could not know these exclusions, being myself neither Christian nor Greek, quite possibly having stripped myself of any specifically human character at all, even as in the certainly non-human I find much that reminds me of men.

Ronald Crane observed that the social sciences are aligning themselves increasingly with humane studies — he did not mean to be invidious in saying that they were becoming more "humanistic." Even so, there are enough investigators in the various fields still working at cross-purposes to make it evident that for many communication has become impossible. Specialization estranges, and the philosophic foundations upon which the specialities are built are too often lost to view. They are not merely ignored for the reminder of the need to examine them is commonly met with scorn. The jibe — "the new clericalism" — is too often deserved. Yet I believe that social scientists show more interest in searching for the means of harmonizing and coordinating all studies of human matters than do the professors of the humanities. The issues are extremely difficult to resolve, deriving of course from what science has been taken to be since "the Cartesian revolution." But the efforts are being made, there are some impressive successes, and so there is hope, for reaching agreements and discovering the means of serving common ends.

As an ordinary traveller, not a scientist, I am prepared for the strange in whatever out of the animal kingdom comes before me. I am likely enough to be hostile, and I interpret my hostility to be as just a judge as the affection I feel for other strange creatures. But whatever the differences in my feelings, as a layman I am always expecting to discover bonds with those I meet, and the more I am in their company the more I look for likenesses, and for even the slightest ways in which we might, as it were, change places. As Hooker said, the traveller looks to overcome hostility, and to be rewarded with amity.

If soon enough biology entices the scientific traveller, and his observations encourage him in the study of genetics, and notions of heredity and of origins lead him towards metaphysical and religious propositions, if he raises his sights to take in the study of the processes by which the people he studies have become what they are, he will still to the very last maintain the attitude of someone outside the objects of his observation. He will preserve to the last the conviction, one might say the solace, of being external, of, in fact, being alien to his subject. He will deny and if he can he will refute precisely what Terence is asserting with such confidence, he will insist on alienation as the mark of his own probity, and the means of the confirmation of his conclusions.

The paradox for both scientist and layman now leaps out at us — how can we know the alien except through degrading ourselves — endeavoring some impossible abdication to become a wholly abstract observer, degraded to the very identity of the aboriginal and bestial, even the vegetable, following the lead of fiction writers — it may be Kafka, for example, and Burgess — all who take their clues from the determination to alienate thought from sympathy?

It may be that the current high standing of the social sciences owes more to the intellectual climate than to remarkable successes either in explaining the unexplained or in providing solutions to problems, theoretical or practical. The dominance of positivism in recent times together with the diminished authority of rationality and tradition makes it obligatory to accept respectfully whatever presents itself in one sense so unpretentiously and yet with so high a regard for exactness. These studies are alluring by the very fact that, disavowing doctrinal or dogmatic authority, they nevertheless promise to encompass all knowledge bearing on human concerns.

These sciences cover matters that are by no means fixed within precise boundaries, nor is there general understanding of the means of coordinating the different techniques that warrant their character as sciences. Yet the general category is meaningful, and it serves well enough to distinguish them from humanistic studies as these are commonly understood — linguistics, literary and artistic criticism, history, and philosophy.

The distinction is pointedly made in the title of a recent anthology, *The Proper Study of Mankind*. For many decades the phrase has carried the meaning Alexander Pope gave it, signifying that humans are to look for help in our efforts to understand manners and morals in literature and history and philosophy, depending no more than Socrates on the study of nature and the physical world. This book, however, is a collection of sociological writings in which the illumination offered is based upon the study of human activities carried forward through methods borrowed from the physical sciences, treating their subjects as those sciences do. The title is plainly intended to pre-empt the claims of traditional studies to sufficiency if not to utility.

In representing the social sciences the contributors to the volume adhere to the now established conventions, cultivating attitudes as objective as those maintained in the study of matter and energy, and referring all to fact. They commonly present the results of their investigations soberly; all the same they are confident of the rigor with which they have conducted their analyses, and they look towards the reader's scrutiny with evident assurance.

78

There are among social scientists, such as those represented in this volume, who question the validity of many of the customary practices. "We [sociologists] are the victims of a naïve quest for 'ultimate objectivity.' It is this crude objectivism — which belongs to our inferiority complexes *vis à vis* the physical sciences — that helps to explain, in turn, the lasting popularity not only of Marx but of social Darwinism, i.e., the idea that man is a creature of his environment. . . . Perhaps the most prevalent sociological conception of man is that which views him as primarily a product of socialization in every society. Man's original nature is thus seen as neither good nor evil, social nor unsocial, but rather as representing the potential that can be molded and shaped to several societal requirements and given various types of content." There are those who push the positivist approach to the extreme: "We must be able to show that symbols such as honor, duty, loyalty, etc., and the behavior which they represent are as observable and objective data as are baseball, the seasonal flight of birds, or the jump of an electric spark." There are some who may be said to evade the issues: "Inner-feelings and thoughts cannot be measured or weighed; they cannot be centrifuged or photographed, chromotographed, spectographed, or otherwise recorded or dealt with objectively by any scientific methodology. As some kind of introspective, private, inner something, accessible only to the one experiencing individual, they simply must be excluded by policy from any scientific model for scientific explanation."

It is to be expected that Marxists would be among those most critical of studies aspiring to a scientific character when circumscribed and directed by positivist doctrine. But when allowance is made for Marxist bias in his commitment to economic determinism, Lucien Goldmann's judgment on this point seems to me to be unexceptionable: "Instead of the implicit or explicit unanimity of value-judgements about the research and the adequate understanding which are found at the basis of the physio-chemical sciences, we encounter, in the human sciences, fundamental differences of attitude existing at the start, prior to the work of research, which often remain implicit and unconscious. This is why objectivity is here no longer a simple, individual problem; it is no longer merely a question of intelligence, penetration, intellectual honesty and other qualities or defects of the individual. Undoubtedly the individual can transcend the horizon of his class and accept points of view which correspond to the interests and values of another class if this new position permits him better to understand the facts; he may even — the individual not necessarily being consistent — preserve old values and acknowledge truths which are unfavourable to them. But those are relatively rare exceptions, and usually the thinker accepts, in completely good faith, the implicit categories of a mentality which, from the start, shuts him off from the understanding of an important part of reality.''[1]

In the end, however, I believe it is the layman, free from the constraints imposed by theory, depending on normal conscientiousness and mother wit, who will arrive at more generally acceptable results. Herodotus, of course, was a man of most remarkable powers of mind, but one need not be a scientist to understand and weigh his interpretations. It is in this conviction that I offer comment on a distinguished modern work that as far as I may judge asks to be considered as we consider his.

This is a collection of sociological essays on the ways of honor and shame in the Middle East.[2] It exhibits the results of patient and conscientious investigations, inspiring faith in the analyses, gaining my confidence by their evidently scholarly character. I came to grant these papers "scientific" status, for the doctrinaire was avoided, and the reasoning gained the approbation of sense.

The collection has to do with a number of groups of people in this region, Berbers, Orthodox Christians in certain ethnic communities, Jews. The representation of the traditional teachings of these peoples, the analyses of opinions and attitudes, the descriptions of behavior were full enough to carry authority, and they were clear and spare. The authors were as pointed in discriminating between differences as in noting similarities, and the carefully controlled generalizations bring forth in a reader's mind speculations that seem particularly useful because they are occasioned by such obviously disciplined observation.

But the work became more and more meaningful to me as it came to be something more than a work of objective science. At point after point I found myself weighing the character of the minds of the authors as they made their observations, as I found them setting one category of observation against another. After a while, it became obvious that the sentences were expressing not only facts but the intelligences of the authors, informed by moral concerns they shared not only with their subjects but with me, a chance reader.

I became convinced that the writers' own thinking about honor and shame had been formed by western traditions, even that they had been influenced by particular ideas that might have come from Shakespeare's play about a noble Moor and sacrificial murder and shame that burned a man like gulfs of liquid fire. The paraphernalia of questions and answers, the recording and interpreting of the statistics, were assimilated in assertions that held my attention because they revealed that the writers themselves knew the meaning of honor and shame, knew the value of the one and the harm of the other, had felt them as I did. And quite apart from any actions a Berber, say, would take out of self-respect or in revenge, when sheep had been stolen, or wife ravished, or children slain, these twentieth-century English writers through the discriminations in their descriptions and analyses reveal that they acknowledged like imperatives for themselves. They supposed these Berbers, like themselves, would have responded as we see Macduff did; learning of the slaughter of his wife and children he was stunned at first, and then questioned on his silence and petrifaction, and called upon to

Dispute it like a man,

said, as we sense these writers would also say,

I shall do so.
But I must also feel it as a man.
I cannot but remember such things were
That were most precious to me. Did Heaven look on
And would not take their part?

The book is, I am confident, an addition to knowledge, it tells us about samenesses and differences among particular peoples and within particular traditions. Much is positivistic science, but much is suggestion. The descriptions merging into explanations, these merging into the ascription of causes, yet look beyond what science would certify. And any reader, I believe, must acknowledge that the value of the work lies at least as much in the intuitive and the critical as in the arrangement of data — intuitions and judgments that could only be referred to fellow-feeling, never to observation uninstructed by feeling. Such an effect depends on an approach science should be glad to authorize, but in common practice it would be abjured. The reader of such a study grants agreement because he is being reminded of what he already knows, reminded that what he observes in others he is able to observe because he already knows of it within himself. As these new particulars are presented to him, in imagination he puts himself in the position of those he is being told of. It is the special excellence of this study that the data have been so organized that a reader's sympathies are being exploited without being imposed upon.

Not many behavioral studies are managed with the tact and presented with the insight that distinguish this, for the overwhelming number do depend on assumptions and ideas that the data, left to themselves, will not express.

In a vitally important respect these contributors have prejudged the matter, assuming dispositions in those they were observing to be like those they knew within themselves. This went so far that it seemed to me they discovered significant differences only in the modes of behavior, not in the impulses or the ends. They assumed a common humanity, and all was seen in the light of such a reference. And as someone following their accounts, not in the light of any comparable experience of my own, but detached and critical as anyone who does not wish to be fooled, I concluded that the fundamental commitment of these writers was inherently less objectionable than one resting on the idea of a disembodied analyst, the usual norm of positivist studies.

One may imagine other studies in which reference to the sensibilities and approval and disapproval of the authors would be so thoroughly repressed that the account of the ways of honor and shame would be presented with the aridity — to borrow an old phrase in order to extend its force — of the dismal science itself. And if this aridity should put me off I might conclude that this is as it should be, that Eliseo Vivas is right when he says that we eviscerate intellection in attempting to divorce perception from understanding.

It may be that in following the prescription for a perfectly value-free perspective we but teach bloody instructions to return upon the inventor, that this unnatural profession corrupts judgment: "Cultural relativism . . . seeks to reduce anxiety by viewing cultural data in a human vacuum. . . . This purposive augmentation of the social distance between the anthropologist and the natives he studies enables him to ignore his own anxieties by studying their culture as though culture did not affect human lives."[3]

But there may be another fault, likewise unacknowledged, inherent in the original motivation — the intrusion from the start of the intent to advance human well-being.

This writer approaches the issue gingerly: "Economics, sociology or any social science . . . work in the indicative, not the ethical, optative mood. As sciences they cannot lay down the ultimate aims or ends of society, however measurable these aims may be. To be practical, the social sciences, though they cannot as sciences determine what is welfare, must take account of the public opinion which, in a democratic country, will be needed to implement their conclusions. They must recognize if not the aims, at least the aversions of the people with whom they are concerned."[4]

Another theorist is obviously straining at the leash, not content to accept the restraints positivism imposes, resisting the appeal "to cause" in order to refuse the temptation to identify "prediction" with "ends": "The discovery of patterns, the calculation of risks, of inductive generalization, and the making of reasonably accurate predictions regardless of the appropriate causal theory have become accepted statistical tasks of data 'elucidation' and 'analysis.'"

Here is one who speaks with such complacency that benevolence is allowed to identify learning with mental health in the very terms we meet with in more than one college announcement: "If the conception of the therapeutic community is to be successfully redefined, there will have to be significant changes in the training of behavioral and humanistic scientists and in the role played by them in society. . . . If the university is to be successfully transformed from a learning factory into a therapeutic community, those who plan and direct the transformation must be familiar with psychiatric methods and insights. Decisions about curricular and degree requirements, the design of buildings and physical settings to provide the necessary means of privacy and collegiality, rules and regulations, students and faculty housing arrangements, and much else — these decisions require more than the part-time consultative services of a social psychiatrist or clinical psychologist. Ideally those who make these decisions will be generalists, not specialists, and as generalists they will be participant-observers in therapeutic processes that draw on the whole range of the behavioral and humanistic scientists.''

In addition to the inconsistencies occasioned by the neglect of the ''anxieties'' of the observer, and by the opposite, the intrusion of benevolence, there is what is probably the more damaging factor, the submission to ''the indicative,'' all study being confined to the single dimension of the present. The hegemony of memory is denied at every step — the point is made in psychological rather than philosophic terms by George Devereux: ''Behavioral science is less scientific than is physics or biology . . . because physical phenomena are determined by a small number of relatively easily quantifiable variables, while the behavior of man can be understood only in terms of a very large number of variables. Moreover, a reasonably complete knowledge of the state of a physical system at time t usually enables one to predict its state at time $t + \Delta t$, whereas, in order to predict man's behavior at time $t + \Delta t$, one must know his state not only at the preceding moment t, but also throughout his life, since man is a chronoholistic system, whose behavior is more far-reachingly determined by a type of 'memory' somewhat resembling hysteresis in physics, than by his current state and situation.''[5]

Positivism, although so generally supplying the underpinning of the social sciences, is so often essentially compromised that one might sometimes believe it was being disowned. This is most apparent when the success in discovering generalizations — ''inductive generalizations'' — is taken to justify attributing to them the standing attained by laws in the physical sciences. But a more common, nearly universal appeal comes through the testings that invite dependence upon the pragmatic, and so lead to the cultivation of empirical philosophy. This is so notable a development that far from compromising the initial procedures and practices it may be thought to have provided the means of superseding them: ''The whole concern over the scientific status of sociology may be irrelevant. Progress in the field does not depend upon its validation and acceptance as a natural science but rather depends upon the accumulation of specific, empirical studies in various areas of social life. Such research, *in toto,* will contribute to man's understanding of his place in society and will add to his social and cultural awareness concerning his relationships with his fellows and his role in the social system.''

Pragmatism, of course, stakes everything on efficacy, disavowing any appeal to an order in nature or to rationality, depending solely on what in experience proves to be manageable. Although pragmatism is of course vulnerable as an intellectual system when confronted with the unmanageable, it shares with positivism the appeal to the apparently concrete, to the here-and-now, to observable data, and whether consistently with it or not it abets positivism in presenting social science as science. The study of "the mechanism of perception" is proposed as a means of "conflict resolution." The procedures are of course complex in so ambitious an undertaking but the formulas are equal to the blueprint: "Cross-cultural studies of the socialization process and developments in personality theory promise to yield information that will increase our ability to predict behavior in the field of international events." The thesis is that scientists will obtain the information required to enable them to predict how a particular government at a particular time will act when faced with a particular problem. This knowledge will of course not be knowledge that will be valued for its own sake, it will be put to the service of someone or other who then will make use of it in coping with the decisions that are being made or are about to be made. Which is to say that the temptation to put this knowledge to use is irresistible, but what is of special relevance in this discussion is that social scientists feel justified in moving from the capacity to predict to acts of intervention apparently because the scientific endeavor is benevolently inspired. The notion that the disinterested search for truth is a good thing as it were automatically carries with it the belief that the truth gained in the hands of its discoverers will be well applied in accordance with the very nature of the method that was followed in reaching it.

As I see it, the ardor with which social scientists follow their studies by recommendations for use is pitched so high that they commonly fail to distinguish between the desire to do good and the desire for power for its own sake. The determination on the part of many to put their discoveries to use goes so far that even opportunism is welcomed: "[We] must recognize if not the aims, at least the aversions of the people with whom they are concerned."

In short, the procedures followed so faithfully in excluding ideas of inherent value, leading to generalizations otherwise comprehensive, persuade the investigator that the motives that have produced such results must themselves be inherently good. And all too often one meets with the tone of self-congratulation — the blamelessness of the method reflects the virtuousness of the practitioner.

And then it apparently follows — the entire undertaking being disinterested — the investigator, having no designs upon his human subjects, yet has their good in view. This becomes evident through the over-riding obligation to generality. As in all science the aim is the discovery of regularity. Care for the individual, the notice of idiosyncrasy, dissolves in the regularity that is translated as "stability," "health," "peace," "conflict resolution." Left at this the moralizing might be relatively quiescent, but with the discovery of regularity prediction becomes possible, and indeed an instrument of verification. With the power of prediction comes the inclination to control: a place of learning seen to be a therapeutic institution, all efforts must be made to see that it remains so. Two weeks of programming can de-program a homosexual, therefore — or, more ingratiatingly, "It is to be hoped that long familiarity with the new ideas will save all but the unalterably orthodox from risking marriage between virgins." (*Pace* Coomaraswamy — this from a UNESCO study addressed to the whole world.)

It is often pointed out that social scientists rather frequently become the happiest and most confident of Big Brothers. In this role they have not only the assurance of unimpeachable techniques of analysis, their positivism (a guarantee of integrity by virtue of its eschewal of dogma) and the pragmatism (a guarantee that no selfish designs are controlling the conclusions) unite to sustain the idea of social and mental health as a knowable and manageable universal good.

One can hardly overestimate the social scientist's dependence upon ideas of well-being and health and upon the conviction of his own good-will and capacity to effect good things. If in his studies he is supported chiefly by positivist philosophy, it is to be understood that this will give him no reason for discovering evil in anything; positivism knows neither good nor evil, but for some reason an *ignorance* of evil allows him to posit the existence of good. There is sometimes a sort of way out which appears to be cynical, for when the health of the society is determined, as it so commonly is, to be a democratic state, this may not turn out to be identical with the results social planning is expected to achieve. Then, one may be led to say, "Trying to find a balance of net advantages between industrial democracy and efficiency certainly involves integration of sociological and economic research and will probably result in a compromise degree of democracy and efficiency." Here, it appears, democracy is being sustained at a cost that is rather regretted.

In drawing upon a variety of sources to outline what I believe to be dominating assumptions and directions in the social sciences, I have of course, both directly and indirectly, put forward a criticism of the aspirations towards objectivity in the study of human affairs and in part of the aims to which the social scientists commit themselves, sometimes openly, somethings covertly. There is nothing original in this criticism, it is being made in many quarters, and I am summarizing but part of it, in order, of course, to begin to make a case for other kinds of study that may in the long run be of greater value. The main and it seems to me inescapable point that such criticism makes is that social scientists cannot afford to pursue their investigations without a serious and sustained effort to found their work in philosophies that stand the test of scrutiny better than positivism or pragmatism in the present state of thought are able to do. The tumult and the shouting is not over with, of course, and positivism in particular is still holding out against the phenomenologists and existentialists and neo-scholastics to mention no others, although its future looks very dim. But positivism pursued philosophically is one thing, supporting the physical and social sciences it is another, and in treating realms in which moral considerations inhere it is evidently susceptible to such incoherence that it serves to discredit undertakings which properly pursued would indeed advance welfare as well as knowledge.

One effort to avoid these contradictions — which it is important to say continues to dominate study after study even though in recent decades social scientists of many persuasions have exposed the inconsistencies and fallacies — has been in the limitations behaviorism promises to set to the extravagant and the non-verifiable. A sustained effort in this direction has evidently fallen into a crucial deficiency of a kind opposite to those I have been pointing to: "Behaviorism in the style of Thurstone was, however, inadequate as a fundamental paradigm for a major social science. Its conception of the scientific method was too narrow, especially in its failure to include systems approaches. Its choice of attitude as the fundamental unit reflected a narrow approach to psychology and proved unsatisfactory to scholars who felt that power, role, socialization, value allocation, or communications, among other concepts, were claimants to the all-important title of political atom."

Here there is the indication of the last refuge of all. I am inclined to believe that it is in desperation that the positivist falls back to seek support in determinism, to the thought, for example, of the political atom, to the thought that all might finally turn out to be another model in the style of the old-fashioned molecular physics. I think this may be desperation engendered by the instability inherent in the Humean flux, by the perception of the complexity that never reveals constant patterns. However this may be, I am more and more impressed by the pervasiveness of the determinism in branch after branch of these studies, the more striking for its naiveté, even for its recourse to mechanistic analogies when from every side the idea of the machine even in the physical world is less and less useful. And despite the observations that I have already drawn attention to, that thoughts and feelings and determinations cannot be weighed, that innumerable factors cannot be quantified, an anthropologist will still say: "Our ideas, our values, our acts, even our emotions, are, like our nervous system itself, cultural products — products manufactured, indeed, out of tendencies, capacities, and dispositions with which we were born, but manufactured none the less."

NOTES

[1] Lucien Goldmann, *The Human Sciences & Philosophy,* London, 1973, p. 40.
[2] Jean G. Péristiany, ed., *Honour and Shame: The Values of Mediterranean Society,* London, 1966.
[3] *From Anxiety to Method in the Behavioral Sciences,* The Hague, 1967, p. 87.
[4] *Ibid.,* p. 4.

Objectivity and Probity

When we pay respect to such power as we have to understand ourselves and to direct our lives we know we must come to terms with all that can undermine this confidence. In crediting the sense of solidarity and purpose that attends the delights accruing to communication and the arts we know we must learn how to confront what would disprize the value we believe they have for us. The existence of an entity called the self, the idea of autonomy, the conviction of communication, all may be brought into question, not only by philosophy but also by what eludes the kinds of confirmation analysis suggests in other areas of experience. The questions are sharp and subtle, raising philosphic issues concerning the nature of existence as well as the nature of knowledge. Challenges come from traditional scepticism, reinforced by the developments Descartes inspired. The advances made by the physical sciences in using assumptions and methods his work authorized encourage the study of human affairs in ways as close as may be to those proven useful in the study of the inanimate.

Traditional ideas on the nature of the self, on the autonomy of humans, on communication, have always referred to ideas of purpose, of inherent worth, of ideas of reality that scepticism questions. So much that had been insisted upon in the past is not "observable," and thus it has seemed proper to exclude from the consideration of human matters what, when excluded from the consideration of all else, was leading to such impressive results. The questions being searching, the controversy was impassioned, — the old phrase, "The Warfare of Science and Theology," points to the understanding that on the key issues there could be no compromise.

Confined to narrow categories the quarrel cannot be settled, but when the faiths and procedures sustaining the sciences and the arts are brought forward for the examination, the possibility arises that metaphysics may provide an accommodation, perhaps even a radical resolution of the issues. On neither side in the current intellectual climate is the invitation to such an endeavor enthusiastically accepted. Yet in a number of developments among theorists of science as among some reasoning on aesthetics and language, among phenomenologists and existentialists (the list could go on), the possibility of rapprochement becomes apparent. One thing is certain — the usual impasse is grievous, leading so many to develop their thought, as Owen Barfield illustrated so well in *Worlds Apart,* quite out of touch with so many others.

Instead of looking forward to cooperation among physicists, sociologists, theologians, historians, we may look to increasing estrangement, the knowledge in the various fields so opaque to those deep in their specialites that it seems hopeless to look for a common ground. Yet the various specialists require and demand protection which they are so far able to count on from universities. For a variety of reasons these require a gathering place, and some need the support of others in pursuing their own work. Yet it is obvious that specialization puts obstacles in the way of communication, and professionalism also favors any indisposition to subordinate particular interests to general ends. For many it is enough if there is an understanding that their own specialty is tolerated, and the justification of an institution becomes the capacity to entertain diversity. A rote appeal is still made to the cohesiveness that maintained the character of the ancient universities and academies, and to freedom from restraint, but in accordance with the postulates supporting most modern specializations it might be more fitting to make the appeal in the name of license. Objectivity maintained in the study of language, morals, physics, medicine — all subjects — defines the temper of the whole, all depending, of course, on the integrity with which each discipline is sustained.

There have been of course substantial refinements and modifications in furthering the approaches Descartes formulated, but the essential attitude remains the same. As clear an expression of this as any is this that Freud at one time set down: ''Scientific thought extends its interest to things which have no immediate obvious utility, it endeavors to eliminate personal factors and emotional influences. Its aim is to arrive at correspondences with reality, that is to say with what exists outside and independently of us. This correspondence with the real extended world we call truth." And then it becomes the endeavor to search "the world inside" in order to demonstrate just such regularities as are observed "outside."

We remain trapped in the dilemma because we are bound to approve the remarkable results science has achieved in following the objectivist mode. Trapped because these procedures exclude any consideration of purpose or end and yet arrive at results that often make human well-being possible. But such an end is not properly to be proposed in the investigation into the nature of things and will only be put forward as the investigation is concluded. To rehearse briefly the essential matter, purpose is not observable, although change may be inferred. Activity, mechanisms, subsidings and transformations, are patterns thrown up out of unending flux, in time to dissolve in flux, meaninglessly. But for the while the patterns are discernible and translatable into formulas they become the instruments of the power that we exercise either compulsively, as an extension of the energy that has led to the undertaking, or in the pursuit of further understanding — in either instance, as the ineluctable condition of our existence, as instinctual as breathing.

But another question also arises — what are the inducements or compulsions of power, leading us to function in accord with the "conditions" of existence? What is the effect for the individual in compliance? What are the effects of an indisposition to comply? The usual answer is no doubt tautological — that energy and therefore power is its own excuse for being. This is fair enough as far as it goes yet not everyone lends himself to be an instrument of power, and those who do and do so most effectively do so through intent, discipline, and sacrifice. Again and again they display character at its most admirable, carrying on work through resolution and unsparing commitment. A certain school might traduce this as "programmed," but to others it appears perfect dedication risking futility in facing every challenge, as confident in submission to law in failure as in success. The judgment René Nelli passed upon Jacques Monod's determinism may be extended: Monod, he said, ended with the conclusion reached by the Manichaeans, that there are two powers sharing the universe, one good, one evil; one conforming to the observable behavior of machines, the other stubborn and intractable. Matter and nature are in the resistless power of the evil, reasonable god, spirit in the hands of the ineffectual. For those who follow one, "The Kingdom," for the others, "Darkness" — the labels are Monod's.

Many have objected to the part Descartes gave the soul in managing the machine and in the interest of consistency have undertaken to exorcise "the ghost." If this crucial difficulty is as unsettling as ever there is another as consequential. The cult of objectivity fosters a contrarious disposition in the consciousness of its practitioners; it may even , in what may not be a metaphor, require the positing of a fission in the analytical agency, the brain. However this may be, it is not only that we do not live in the world in which we think, it is, more ruinously, that we feel bound to commit ourselves to this division in our lives — it becomes, ironically, a point of integrity to insist on the schism. The conflict, and the knowledge of it, undermines, of course, the possibility of harmony in our sensibilities and of coherence in our thought — we are to be detached in mutilating ourselves and in contemplating the mutilation. We are to pursue a course not too unlike Falstaff's in disowning the claims of honor — eloquent in his high time in defining it as mere breath, in the end reduced to "babbling." For us, a life of focussed purposelessness. The efforts of Karl Popper to resolve the dilemma have been characterized as a less than plausible Platonism.[1]

There is no possible reconciling of oppositions that have gone this far but in that final reduction one recognizes the urgency of the need to discover the procedures by which we may concede all that is necessary to a view of things in which assumptions of the purposeless and the valueless lead to such triumphs over matter and energy while defending the one proposition that limits the realm in which such operations are acceptable. The accomodation evidently depends on honoring the need of humans to maintain the probity of reason while maintaining the possessions of a degree of freedom, of some power not wholly subject to laws of mechanics. Endowed with the power of choice the individual by making preferences determines ends in the light of fore-conceived purposes. There is law well enough, and he is subject to it, but he has a variety of ways of observing it: through compliance or in

92

rebellion he will give witness to its power and efficacy. But when he observes it in honoring it, and does so freely, and towards certain ends, his freedom is enlarged. The religious will be able to say with the Prayer Book, "In Thy service is perfect freedom." As in all other works — developing skills, managing arts, training muscles — the observance of the laws, freely and judiciously, is known to magnify the power and the life of the observer of the laws.

In undertaking to resolve the difficulty we wish to prove that just as we entertain a sense of purpose in our living so do we in following the demands of reason; that the idea of probity in following the method of detachment proposed as a self-sufficient end is nonsense, for that probity is attained only through effort, effort that is willed, and in insisting upon this the analyst is referring to a power to which he has granted prior although unacknowledged authority. As I see it, this power functions for him much as for those before Socrates the daimon did that effected communication with the sacred. The obligation for the scientist to refuse to be deceived and above all never to cooperate with deceit lies behind the commitment to objectivity, but the pursuit of objectivity itself is so absorbing that it is all but inevitable that the nature of its dependence upon this prior cult should be forgotten.

The attitude of objectivity is willed. Attention is focused and thereby constricted. Limits are set upon the attention through finite conceptions of time and space. Whatever comes before the attention is reduced to elements that time and space are the bounds for.

By definition focus excludes, and in the attitude of objectivity the willed focus excludes the consideration of wholes as such, being limited to the parts and the relations of the parts to each other, as juxtapositions or sequences. The whole as something other than the congeries of parts — a functioning or growing entity — or as a changing configuration directed by end or purpose — is excluded from consideration. Ultimately, as the analysis of the elements proceeds into the irreducible, consideration even of the coming into being of the elements is foregone. Through such insistence the elements of the animate are regarded as if they were elements of the inanimate, and the question of origin is infinitely deferred. These neglects and exclusions are persisted in because they offer insurance against classifications or generalizations on the part of the observer that are not referrable either to experiment or measurement.

The declared motivation in this rigorous attention to the pursuit of truth is the preservation of the integrity of the observer. Integrity requires the refusal to permit either inclination or method or the deficiencies of evidence to allow for conclusions that are not verifiable in the terms indicated. The appeal to integrity in the observer is in part required by the need for concurrence in the results of the experiments and measurements, an appeal to other observers for whom as well all other considerations than the verification of measure are of no account. But integrity is also required from a firmly held belief in the value of the truths discovered for further explorations. The whole person, in short, is devoted in his activities and in his refusals, to the service not only of the mind but of the possessor of the mind. The positive motive is infinite knowledge; the negative, the fear of deception by what resists measurement, the horror at the self that fosters deception.

And thus the cult of objectivity must run counter to the cult of the self — nowadays, as before by Nietzsche, often written off as "a false Narcissism," — dependence upon a notion of the person as the vessel of truth and meaning. It becomes an effort at dispossession, as if intellect engaged in observation had dispossessed the observer. The effort is pursued furiously, the observer in all the imperfections of his mind and senses being understood to falsify so grievously, to betray reality, reality that only the disembodied mind can be faithful to.

To speak of this as fury appears to prejudice the conclusion. But if the effort is truly unremitting and uncompromising, then by virtue of the implacable rejection of whatever clouds the assurance of certainty, the ascription of fury is called for. Probity, moral perfection, dedication are the very stuff of the undertaking, an undertaking that has disqualified the moral, the upright, the valuable, the personal.

This state founded on a divided disposition, all maintained as it were without regard to the prosperity of the discoverer, all that is gained becoming the property of numberless like discoverers — in this alone is a certain satisfaction and purpose permitted, the satisfaction of participation in the activities of the nameless. The dominant disposition is in the fervor that is as much moral as it is speculative, the fervor in resisting any invitation to relate the discoveries gained to an idea of the purposeful. In refusing the invitation to value himself, and his work as his, he must nevertheless abandon the position of the objective observer in order to serve the cult of objectivity. Perfectly ascetic, he may not justify his asceticism except in passion.

Gilson has called the cult of objectivity "an intellectual asceticism;"[2] Goldmann in the conventional Marxist interpretation refers it to a social base: "It is difficult to see how intellectuals, since they express in their work not only the thought of other groups but also their own *social character as intellectuals* could possess a less subjective point of view than that of any other professional group;"[3] Monod speaks of "the ethical choice:" "True knowledge is ignorant of values, but it cannot be grounded elsewhere than upon a value judgment, or rather upon an *axiomatic* value. It is obvious that the positing of the principle of objectivity as the condition of true knowledge *constitutes an ethical choice and not a judgment arrived at from knowledge, since, according to the postulate's own terms, there cannot have been any 'true' knowledge prior to this arbitral choice.* In order to establish the *norm* for knowledge the objectivity principle defines a *value:* that value is objective knowledge itself."[4] Merleau-Ponty offers a psychological interpretation of its impetus, the persistent animus against those cultivating the sacred: "The eroticism of profanation is too attached to what it negates to become a freedom."[5] There is the point Polanyi makes again and again: "This then is our liberation from objectivism: to realize that we can voice our ultimate convictions only from within our convictions — from within the whole system of acceptances that are logically prior to any particular assertion of our own, prior to the holding of any particular piece of knowledge."[6]

All such criticism commences with the belief that objectivism rests on prior, normally unacknowledged commitments. As with the positivist, who professes no obligation except to what observation makes available, excluding all else — "a collection of prohibitions."[7] The finally telling observation is Polanyi's — what once went properly under the name of scepticism, doubt calling tradition into question, has now become authoritarian: "In the times of Montaigne and Voltaire, rationalism identified itself with doubt of the supernatural, and rationalists called this 'doubt' as opposed to 'belief'. This practice was excusable at the time, since the beliefs held by rationalists — for example, in the supremacy of reason, and in science as an application of reason to nature — had not yet been effectively challenged by scepticism. In propagating their own beliefs the early rationalists were opposing traditional authority on so wide a front that they could well regard themselves as radical sceptics. But the beliefs of rationalism have since been effectively called in question by the revolutionary doctrines of Marxism and Nazism. It is absurd to oppose such doctrines now on the ground of scepticism. For they gained their present ascendancy only recently by a sweeping rejection of Western tradition, and it is rationalism which today relies on tradition — the tradition of the eighteenth and nineteenth centuries — against them. It should also have become clear by this time that the beliefs transmitted by the now imperilled tradition are by no means self-evident. Modern fanaticism is rooted in an extreme scepticism which can only be strengthened, not shaken, by further doses of universal doubt."[8]

In this brief digest of criticism addressed to dedication to objectivity I intend only to point to the range of the criticism now being made increasingly. I do this not to advance the criticism, only as a reminder of the force of the relation of the cult of objectivity to the cult of probity. For in this relationship I think we are again in touch with what Burnet observed, that in antiquity the sciences and the study of human matters were rooted in a common mentality. All thought was referred to the integrity of the human being, an integrity dependent upon belief in the hospitality of the universe. Professor Ballard has pointed to the doctrine in the *Laws* which, I believe, we must appeal to ultimately in refuting the nihilism that exclusive reliance upon value-free objectivity leads to:[9]

> "The ruler of the universe has ordered all things with a view to the excellence and preservation of the whole, and each part, as far as may be, has an action and passion appropriate to it. Over these, down to the last fraction of them, ministers have been appointed to preside, who have wrought out their perfection with infinitesimal exactness. And one of these portions of the universe is thine own, unhappy man, which,

however little, contributes to the whole; and you do not seem to be aware that this and every other creation is for the sake of the whole, and in order that the life of the whole may be blessed; and that you are created for the sake of the whole, and not the whole for the sake of you." (*Laws* 903, tr. Jowett.)

The Delphic oracle gained acceptance in part as the voice of a god, in part through providing guidance in the conduct of affairs. The results of compliance were bound to be mixed, but they were universally reverenced. And so it is with us in cultivating probity — although we may hold back from the appeal to absolute truth and justice — we are bound to honor it as a compelling instruction.

We know too well that the idea of recourse to an inner authority can become an appeal to sensation, to such intuitions as deserve to be called gnostic, to any number of irrational stirrings that lay claim to authority, and therefore what we look for as deserving trust is what rationality can provide in supporting the conviction of our integrity. In short, the testing comes through reason's discovery of order in our dispositions and in our relationships with all else, referring, with Plato, our part to the whole. The root of the word *probity* says it all.

That testing comes in part through self-examination, in part through such concurrence as we may find in the experiences of others. This is no mere appeal to *consensus gentium,* or even to the laws of nature and of nations — the authority of the oracle rests upon such testing as humanity itself approves through an infinite number of expressions — proverbs, wisdom, tradition, above all by those works that in depth and comprehension and beauty establish the character we call classic — manifest in the western world above all else in the *Iliad.* It is through the comprehensiveness of mind made known to us through the arts of expression — even Dryden's phrase, "largest and most comprehensive soul," is too limiting through not stressing intellection enough — that each of us tests his own humanity, and his capacity for wholeness. Throughout history the efforts of humans have been unceasing in the effort to explore the realms of being, light penetrating every observable relationship — Plato, Augustine, Confucius, Dante, Newton, Darwin, Einstein — and in acquaintance with that never-ending history through the words that have come to him each human learns of his own expansiveness as well as of the constancy of the reference he brings to all that comes before him.

NOTES

[1] "The Search for Objectivity in Peirce and Popper," in *The Philosophy of Karl Popper.* ed. P. A. Schilpp, La Salle, 1974, pp. 482 and 496.

[2] *D'Aristote à Darwin et Retour,* Paris, 1971, p. 25.

[3] Lucien Goldmann, *The Human Sciences & Philosophy,* tr. H. V. White and Robert Anchor, London, 1969, p. 52.

[4] *Chance and Necessity,* tr. Austryn Wainhouse, New York, 1971, p. 176.

[5] *Signes,* Paris, 1960, p. 386.

[6] *Personal Knowledge,* Chicago, 1974, p. 267.

[7] Kolakowski, *The Alienation of Reason,* p. 18.

[8] *Personal Knowledge,* p. 298.

[9] E. G. Ballard, *Socratic Ignorance,* p. 156.

Study and Celebration

I

Our enjoyment of the arts, our absorption in records of the past, the excitements of speculation, all help us find our bearings, but it is as satisfactions in themselves that we value them most truly. When we undertake to study what has gone into their making we speak of these as "the humanities." The aims of study are primarily for our instruction, and the old phrasing remains a useful guide — the arts may instruct, but they must delight; study, too, can delight, but it must instruct.

We need to make other discriminations also when certain terms are brought into the discussion of these matters, and this is most particularly true in admitting the term "humanism." It is a quite general practice to associate the humanities with humanism, and the history of education since the Renaissance makes that a natural pairing. But we also know that such a variety of attitudes and philosophic affiliations goes under this name that we may take only a limited aspect of its many meanings if we are not to become confused. More important still, when we are concerned to keep in mind distinctions between the arts of expression and their study we may remember that Homer has never been so valued as in the centuries before we can detect anything like the movements that go by the name of humanism. The key idea relating these terms resides, of course, in the word "human," and the difficulties commence there — with what we may take that to signify.

Many writings on human matters that are offered as sciences

kindle in us respect not too unlike that we pay to works of literature and philosophy although we seldom lose sight of their purposes as science. Reading these — Max Weber and Freud and Raymond Aron — we quickly notice lesser concerns, when there is any at all, for style, for play, for the effects of beauty. These are not the only distinctions, nor the most important, but striking and important enough. What we are accustomed to call the humanities, on the other hand, even works treating matter the sciences would take as theirs, and following the procedures not of imaginative writings but of treatises — *The Prince*, the *Novum Organum*, the *Leviathan* — we call such because the art is the means of carrying the thought farther than would be within the compass of the most faithful paraphrase, it contributes force and stirs resonances not within the capacity of mere statement, whether as description or classification or even in proposing inferences. The manner, the character of the writing and the procedures in ordering the whole, in effect relieve these works of the constraints placed upon writing that is committed to the sparest representation of the truth, to the unclouded mirroring of reality. Such would be the character scientific writing would aspire to.

The form and style of literature, no less seriously devoted to the expression of truth when verisimilitude is at issue, confers upon its material a kind of sufficiency in which the work appears to have the quality of a living entity, to possess an energy and voice of its own. The manner, or the style, appears to effect a change in the matter of the discourse, the matter presented now appearing to possess an import and worth that scientific observation does not account for, or, it may be, even take into view. The writing itself brings into our thoughts something more than the recognition of what it is in reality the words are telling of, it induces in us an awareness of a being and energy we had not been alert to in the matter before us. It is not only that such writing acquaints us with another mind, another scheme of thought, other knowledge and insights, it becomes a manifestation of the power in a human mind to transfer its life to others, to us, to transfer the force in the thought that brought that thought into being, thereby establishing its power over us. Machiavelli acquaints us with a view of things as they possibly are and as we are inclined to acknowledge them to be, but he acquaints us also with the further knowledge that in listening to him we are discovering not only what we had already known but also other ways of looking at the world. In the concurrence as in the surprise, in the delight as in the dismay and incredulity, we find ourselves scrutinizing what he has moved us with, initiating corrections in our thoughts, stimulating hardly dreamed of inferences, and so, captivating. Works of scientific character also propose continuing explorations into truths and hypotheses they apprise us of, but more patiently and trustingly.

Scientific writings that do not possess the character of literature also bear the marks of their authors to varying degrees, but they generally reveal even more of the schemes and methods the investigations are forwarding. They make it their business to take us into their confidence. The methods of science, the schemes developed for the presentation of the procedures of investigation, and the results, are in fact designed to let us know the precise limitations of human intellection. By such means, paradoxically, scientists give the most significant stamp to their work, establishing by this very revelation of limits the claim of the individual scientist's work to authority. Yet in being so precise about their limits even as the scope of their investigation expands, Galileo and Newton and Darwin provoke speculation on the very matters they are intent on excluding. It turns out to be appropriate, in following Galileo's reasoning, to pursue implications into realms he did not enter. But the great differences in the vistas of thought that unfold for the intellect out of scientific truths are in their perfect coherence with their beginnings, the initial formulations justifying perfectly the later ones, a consistency in the description and explanations that depends to an important degree upon the restraints that are imposed upon the character of the observation itself as well as upon the reasoning. The reasoning literature develops looks towards the unnamed, which it is referring to and yet leaves unidentified. In an obvious respect we may say that what most matters in the arts is something other than what is immediately before us. The inferences and the conclusions we are induced to accept through devious and even unlikely tricks rather than through the verification by prediction science provides. The line —

To behold a world in a grain of sand —

appears to indicate a perfectly definable truth, that the smallest things are marvellously complex, and the statement is at once the occasion for conviction, conviction of the truth that there is much to be seen in the little and that this is a matter for wonder. But the special power of the line and of the thoughts it gives rise to comes in eliciting both our concurrence in the ambitiousness of the generalization and equally in the reticence, in the refusal to spell out even one of the multitude of particulars a scientific statement would require us to notice and commence to enumerate. For the poet the idea even of commencing to list the particulars would circumscribe the sense of the greatness and confuse the idea of the smallness of the world he is speaking of. He leaves us free, as Pascal did not, to conceive of the infinite unencumbered, and thus works a stranger, more powerful charm. Science looks for confirmation in pointing to patterns of events that correspond to the patterns of its own reasoning, and the arts look for confirmation in events that fall into patterns that appear to be as irreducible to formulation as the habit of a particular tree or of any form of life, a habit conforming to what we have learned of the species, yet also evidently unique. From a scientific point of view it is dangerously compromising that Hume should depend so much upon the metaphor of the flux, that Lévi-Strauss is so wed to the idea of a center in space, that the metaphors of economics should so serve the thought of Freud, but from the layman's point of view these images provide all but a validation of the rest. Robert Plot in the seventeenth century made a valiant effort to relieve his thought of unwanted burdens: "And these [descriptions] I intend to deliver as succinctly as may be, in a plain, easie, unartificial Stile, studiously avoiding all ornaments of Language, it being my purpose to treat of Things, and therefore would have the Reader expect nothing less than words." He has not hit it quite right, but the intent is clear — he wishes to substitute a schema for reality.

The arts also describe and explain, but the spirit informing them reminds us immediately of the grounds for wonder at what is left unexplained, what may even be unknown. In aspiring to hold our most critical as well as our most rapt attention it reminds us that awe may be as respectful of thought as of facts. What might be plainly and simply scientific in *The Prince* becomes literature as it leads us to entertain the idea that while so much remains to be said it is not necessary to say anything more. We are enticed as much by what is unspoken as by what is pinpointed, and our enjoyment is as much in the suggestion of never-ending surprises with which the thought acquaints as in the precision of what is stated:

"A wise lord cannot, nor ought he to, keep faith when such observance may be turned against him, and when the reasons that cause him to pledge it exist no longer. If men were entirely good this precept would not hold, but because they are bad, and will not keep faith with you, you too are not bound to observe it with them."

We use these discriminations in order to learn what sort of credence we give to the different ways by which human matters are represented by the sciences and the arts and soon enough we recognize that we must consider more than differences in method. The distinction between the humanities and science as such is ancient although the terms of the distinction are far from constant, and it is certain that nowadays there are weighty reasons requiring us to scrutinize all that would preserve it. We need to examine whatever supports the claims of various kinds of reasoning and writing in order to discover how far they deserve our subscription, how their purposes differ, how far their results overlap. We must always remind ourselves that in the West the fundamental distinction between the study of man and the study of nature goes back to a time when it was not possible to think of human activity as the social scientists are currently able to. The primary and ancient distinction rested upon the conviction that it was necessary to think of man differently than of the world around him. There were many reasons for conceiving of human life as inextricably bound up with an animate cosmos, yet for all that there was the insistent demand that we study man's nature by the light of a certain idea of his special character, his special being and essential ends, neither beast nor god. Socrates bequeathed to western thought the idea that science, defined as the knowledge of external nature, was of little use to man's study of himself. Since knowledge of himself was the human's first obligation, the other was to be neglected if not despised since it would distract him from the study that needed all the time and energy there was. The injunctions to seek true knowledge, the knowledge of the Ideas, not resting with opinion; to seek heavenly beauty, not resting with earthly; to pass from watching the shadows on the wall of the cave to contemplating the splendor of reality, all these led with whatever emphases Plato himself might have disowned to a disprizing of science, to the contempt for the world, to the exploration of the resources of the inner life as the direct path to the knowledge of God, of all good. Many modern humanists are commonly committed to the same exclusion and their criticism carries over to a rejection of the commitments scientists have developed in the study of matter and energy when these are applied to humans and human arrangements. The business of humane study becomes partly the study of the nature of man but more centrally the study of the ways of humans in celebration.

Even when in the history of thought it was appropriate to think of mankind as part and parcel of a cosmos itself understood to be an organism, when the idea of the microcosm as a similitude of the macrocosm encouraged humans in affirming the presence of an identical informing power in both, philosophers quite as much as theologians found reason to conceive of the study of the inner life of humans as distinct in kind. The methods of self-knowledge were not to be the methods employed in the study of the elements nor for that matter in establishing philosophies of cosmic harmony or stellar influence or of the world soul. Writers in the Socratic tradition particularly, Plotinus and Augustine and Petrarch for example, contributed immensely to all that warranted the consideration of man as a thing apart. As Plotinus set it forth:

"Man has come into existence, a living being but not a member of the noblest order: he occupies by choice an intermediate rank; still, in that place in which he exists, Providence does not allow him to be reduced to nothing; on the contrary he is ever being led upwards by all those varied devices which the Divine employs in its labour to increase the dominance of moral value. The human race, therefore, is not deprived by Providence of its rational being; it retains its share, though necessarily limited, in wisdom, intelligence, executive power, and right-doing, the right-doing, at least, of individuals to each other — and even in wronging others people think they are doing right and only paying what is due.

"Man is, therefore, a noble creation, as perfect as the scheme allows; a part, no doubt, in the fabric of the All, he yet holds a lot higher than that of all the other living things of earth." (III.ii.9 — Mackenna)

The Copernican revolution and the development of the mathematical point of view are credited with "reading man out of nature," of dissolving not only the grounds of the analogy of the microcosm and macrocosm, but of any supposition of a spirit or soul common to man and nature, of a pneuma or breath, of what in a later age would return to philosophy as "life" or a "life-force." Following upon this conquest one might have thought there would have been the immediate conclusion that, nature being cut off from man, man would have been cut off from nature, his sentience, consciousness, and intellectuality demanding consideration as an entity of a special kind. One might have thought the most pressing conclusion would have been for a return to the study of man as a being governed in part at least by laws other than those governing nature and the cosmos. There were such consequences but the general effect was in the quite other direction, that man, too, might best be understood when his being was thought of as a field of just such forces as were to be seen elsewhere. First, the cosmos was to be thought of as a machine, and then man. So with Descartes, and then the Deists. Then, the cosmos was to be thought of as a field of energy, and man also. So with Hegel and Marx and Freud. So it went, and while there were, and continue to be, quite refractory considerations, the reasons grew for supposing that ultimately man and society and the works of man might be as usefully examined through the same glasses as all else. New materialisms were formed to do the accounting; determinism in particular pervaded study after study, and something called behaviorism drew particular attention to the scientific study of social matters. Man had been read out of the nature that had been thought to be informed with an organic life only to find himself an indistinguishable part of a universe reduced to matter and energy. It was indeed becoming difficult to retain the idea that there was anything distinctively organic — any pattern, any organization at all, was to be translated into a machine, and if anyone were to suppose there was a ghost in it we were quickly enough reminded that we had long since ceased to believe in ghosts.

Students of the arts, still of the Socratic bias, still profess to find in literature and history and philosophy warrant for believing that the central features of human nature are inaccessible to the methods of science, and that the study of man and his works depend finally not so much on a survey of behavior as in the examination of the "inner" life. Observation, description, analysis, classification, all are inadequate in their accounts of what religion and literature and the other arts say is closest to men's bosoms. Hamlet's question to his mother — "How goes it with you, madam?" — was to find any answer there was to find in such speech as humans address to each other when all barriers to intimacy are removed, where there is nothing to be observed. Hamlet anticipated an answer he could have supplied himself yet that he needed from her, and he would have been as right in trusting words as in trusting silence. Analysis could only profane their interchange.

In this view the study of man is best effected in the affirmation of a common cherishing of felt and weighed experience. Then, what experience is, how it can be thought of as common and felt, and what we are to make of it, how to value it, becomes the pressing question — as much as why day is day, night night, or, more particularly — and always at the back of the mind — are we fools to take comfort in clinging to one another, in being delighted with our acquaintanceships, in asking Hamlet's question, and in knowing the answer?

We look for definitions in distinguishing humane from scientific studies, and such as we find are rough enough, although useful, guides. We may begin again with the observation that humane studies comprise those works that in treating human records treat the affairs they tell of as intrinsically important. In that approach the student implies that he himself can vouch for their importance, through sympathy and the power of imagination. Moreover, he pursues his undertaking in order to underwrite the value of what is spoken of. Such records and such studies call upon our attention differently than do studies of external nature, and we attend to them differently. What we have learned to call science, in the study of nature and of the universe, of course bears upon the concerns scientists know as humans, and particularly the demands the mind makes of itself in searching out truth. It similarly interests every scientist in the provocative power it has of suggesting further explorations and of leading his mind on to applications of his knowledge following the interests of power, over the mind and over nature. These are not the interests of assimilation, nor of correlation with all his other interests as a person, and accordingly the stimulus he values in his activity is deliberately restricted, he submerges his appetite for thought and work to the character he proposes to himself as a scientist, which is to say, as no one in particular. He is caught in the paradox, of course, but he is able to live with it so long as he refrains from relating this appetite to his other interests in any significant order, as in a hierarchy of values. Currently scientists almost always insist on restricting professional interests to the pursuit of knowledge itself, which — unless they take Monod's position — they assume to be devoid of moral or aesthetic or metaphysical significance. Pascal might call attention to the vastness of the universe in order to inspire humility, a modern astronomer must eschew that concern.

In other times, when philosophy had more reason than now to assert that men and nature shared in common purposes, science — biology, physics, astronomy — absorbed men's attention in much the same way as did the study of letters. Even Galileo was certain he was right in likening the *Book of Nature* to God's Book, and the study of the universe was just such an activity as the study of the Bible. The study of the elements and of the stars was in effect the study of texts, the mind in exploring physics presumably following such rules as governed philology. However soon the analogy would be understood not to hold, the disposition was strong to regard all that came before the mind to be instinct with purpose and directed towards an end. But since Descartes, and most especially since the rise of positivism, science has come to be universally regarded as the study of fact and truth, known in advance to bear no witness either to purpose or end. The injunctions of Bacon were obeyed — the Idols were exorcised, and neither language nor philosophy nor the illusions the senses were continually creating would be allowed to confuse the intellect. And even, in the last century or so, when scientists came to acknowledge the impossibility of perfect objectivity, taking account of the influence of the observer upon the matter of his observation, they have by no means returned to introducing into their cogitations the factor of sympathy so many of their predecessors, in antiquity and even in the Renaissance, took for granted as inherent in the nature of their undertakings. Nowadays, of course, it would be a rare investigator who would claim to detect in the matters he was singling out for study the presence of evidence for an author, and nature, almost all are persuaded, has no more of the human in it than of the divine. What the scientist studies is so to speak exterior to him, he confers even upon his analysis of himself the character of externality, and for all he knows, all is as external to any gods that may be. The wheel has made a strange turn, and Galileo's formula has become applicable in a sense contradicting his essential faith — the study of humans and their works, of their writings and all the arts, quite as much as of their dispositions and acts, is just such an undertaking as the study of the material world. Thus it is that the study of man has become a science.

A notion of the external, of what is supposed to possess a character independent of the fears and hopes and wishes humans are always disposed to allow to qualify their reasoning, is the necessary condition of objectivity. We are enjoined not to acknowledge the care we feel for ourselves and our prosperity, and to exclude all those inferences and values and beliefs and superstitions we cultivate in supporting a sense of our individual importance. We are permitted to make no more claims upon the world and the universe than upon unseen powers.

Those pursuing humane studies properly claim to as much rigor and probity as scientists, professing as strong a determination to resist delusion, but while they argue for the need to get outside themselves as cogently as do the scientists, to maintain the detachment that will forestall prejudice, they mean by this something quite different. In their examinations these scholars may defer but they will not exclude the interest in the utility of all that comes before them. That utility is not normally thought of as to be made manifest in act, normally, rather, in assessment and in establishing the disposition for action. The consideration of Hecuba in exile, of Euripides' own bias, of the particular perspectives offered in the Japanese production of *The Trojan Women* — all these and other matters the student weighs by imagining himself in the position of Hecuba and Euripides and the play's producer, all in order to help answer the question — what is there in all this for me? What good is Greek to me? What good is *hoti's* business? The answer he looks to is provided quite simply in the refreshment of his spirits and the encouragement to excellence.

But more than that, too, for when the scholar in the humanities addresses himself to his subject he does so in quite another sense than Ryle meant in speaking of a "ghost" in the "machine." He finds himself engaged in conversation. Humane study is ineluctably informed by the conviction of mutual exchanges, of participation in the lives and concerns and purposes of others. A whole world peopled the study Machiavelli retired to. He had been discharged from his office in the Florentine government, and he was living in near-poverty on a farm. Returning each day from work in the fields he would retire to a small room to read Tacitus, Livy, all the books he loved and was learning from, and he wrote of the evenings he spent there in this way: "On the threshold I slip off my day's clothes with their mud and dirt, put on my royal and curial robes, and enter, decently clothed, the ancient courts of men of old, where I am welcomed kindly and fed on that fare which is mine alone, and for which I was born: where I am not ashamed to address them and ask them the reasons for their actions, and they reply considerately; and for two hours I forget all my cares, I know no more trouble, death loses its terrors: I am utterly translated in their company."

Sometimes one's fellows are coevals but one of the most valued of all experiences comes when we establish community with those of other times and places, across the barrier of time especially. Shakespeare's line which tells of his willingness to depart from life —
Save that to die I leave my love alone —
heartens us in the knowledge that this is our feeling, too, in this present time, we cherish it because it strengthens us in our belief that despite all changes since, changes that we comprehend so dimly, something as central as this loyalty remains exactly the same. When the ancient poet said his words would live forever on men's lips he expressed the truth that out of evanescent breath words, that transmit sense and wisdom and beauty, belong to the life of all those to whom speech has been given.

To point the contrast with such a view of the continuing life of humans by analysis which disposes of the "ghost" one may notice a common enough view of the nature of things much science would accept:

The atmosphere is a medium. A medium permits more or less unhindered movements of animals and displacements of objects. This is what is meant by "space." But a medium has other equally important properties. It also permits the flow of information. It permits the flux of light, it transmits vibration, and it enables the diffusion of volatile substances. Only by illumination do animals "see" things, only by vibration do they "hear" things, and only by diffusion do they "smell" things.

Such is the physical basis of the types of flow of stimulus from a source in the distant environment to the position of a sentient animal. Most of what is broadcast by a light-emitting or light-reflecting source, or a noisy or an odorous source, is never picked up at all; it is wasted for purposes of stimulation. But a set of perspective projections, or a field of sound waves, or the diffusion field of a volatile substance, is a perfectly objective, physical fact.

What is insisted on here is not the constancy of the elements of the human state but of the ways of the elements of the universe, the unending series of causes and effects in a colorless and soundless effluvium (the sense of touch alone is allowed as reference).

Thus again — positivism, determinism, behaviorism — reducing what others may call communication to atomistic and statistical terms — reveal how much obligations to particular philosophies determine the nature of the opposition to the classical humanists. And by that fact they call attention to the need for those who turn to the humanities in countering what they find unsatisfactory in this reductionism to bring forward philosophic support that will not only obtain more general acceptance but that will square with the claims made for the humanities in the past. What is at issue for the scientists in coming to terms with origins and the nature of the interest in objectivity, is equally so for the humanists. With nothing that is human alien to them humanists are all but compelled to be eclectics in philosophy, but there is a limit to their freedom. They are committed to the discovery of order, to obtaining knowledge of order, to assessing celebrations of order. They are, in short, obliged to give reasons for their faith. If they fail in this, for them the arts will be as empty as the studies they make of them.

In the Renaissance the key assertion of the humanists again and again was that freedom conferred a distinctive dignity upon human beings — in freely choosing, discriminating, and acting men could fulfill their potentialities for goodness and greatness. Petrarch had said, "I read in order that I may become better." That is one side of it. The other is as Hamlet put it: "What a piece of work is man, how noble in reason, how infinite in faculties, in form and moving how express and admirable, in action how like an angel, in apprehension how like a god." These faculties, this reason, enabled men to free themselves from the entanglements of the body and of the world, to become better, to be thought of as

110

god-like. What Hamlet speaks of as "apprehension" is in effect celebration, what follows upon thought that is able to range freely, to discover the wondrous.

The postulate is developed that humans, freely judging, possessing the power to govern themselves, at least partly, through reason, are dependent on the knowledge and wisdom that language communicates and letters have preserved. When these humanists undertook to educate they were undertaking to initiate pupils into the traditions sustaining government.

The basic postulate does honor to the individual capacity for forming judgments even as the study of language and literature — the essential arts for these purposes — points to what is owed to tradition. Educational programs were to provide succeeding generations with a knowledge of their debts to the past and this required sustained application over a period of years. In certain areas, in logic and rhetoric in particular, it was necessary to advance towards mastery by carefully articulated stages. Just as a pianist is free to perform expressively only after mastering techniques and after assimilating the lessons of the past, so all those entrusted with responsibility. Men think freshly and freely as they have learned to clear obstructions from their minds, often through systematic processes, and only then can act with the support that will enable them to work towards distant goals.

Such programs were often aimed at educating those who were to be the governors of society although this would not remain the exclusive principle. But in one sense this aristocratic emphasis persists in every development of the idea of humane education in that it keeps one matter clearly at the front of the entire enterprise — the idea of the dignity that distinguishes free men from slaves. The republicans addressed in the American *Federalist Papers* were to cultivate such a sense of self-sufficiency as distinguished the princes and patricians of the Renaissance, following the model established by the ancient Roman rhetoricians. The reasoning was, and is, that even men innately fit to rule, or who through circumstance would be led to, through study would gain improved understanding of the means of stabilizing power. Through disciplined study of the ways of thought that language in its most expert expression acquainted them with they would be the better able to assess the circumstances they were confronting and to assess the means they had of coping with them. Directly and indirectly the texts of Homer and Livy and Cicero would be their counsellors, and children being prepared to rule over the years would have their thoughts grounded in the reasoning of those before them who had encountered such matters as fortune might have in store for anyone. They would learn something of the relation of individuals to peoples and classes. They would learn something of the value and the limits to the uses of force, they would even come to learn of the vanity of power. In learning of the failures as well as the successes of the great they would come to understand the demands that would be made of them. And accordingly the emphasis in education was upon the texts that whether as fiction or history inducted the student into the company of the noble.

Nowadays conceptions of mankind, of a common humanity, of universal patterns in government, and of the authority of reason are not so easily consulted as when philosophers and theologians could successfully defend ideas of a hierarchical universe. The theory of evolution as well as many of the postulates of recent theorists in science make it difficult to determine the boundaries separating humans from non-humans, and even for those still intent upon a celestial hierarchy the problems remain. Any one of us may believe that the painters of the Lasceaux caves were such humans as ourselves but we are far from certain what we mean by that, and with living aborigines we may doubt our ability to communicate to them our inmost thoughts whatever the Rorschach tests tell us; to expect anything like a satisfying answer to Hamlet's question. Nor, of course, is rationality itself allowed a place of privilege in a hierarchy that corresponds to an order in nature and in the universe.

But again — the essential postulate is that reason operates in humans freely, it enables them to judge freely, it alone, functioning freely, gives humans warrant to believe they may advance their state, individually and collectively, from the general enthrallment to chance and fate. Such pride may have led men to impiety — as in the words of the chorus in *Antigone* — ''There is nothing beyond man's power'' — although Prometheus was not wrong —

I showed men the use of reason, I revealed the risings and the settings of the stars so they could understand them, the art of numbers, too, and the most excellent learning of all, the craft and use of writing. I revealed to them the art of memory, the progenitor of poetry.

The fact is that as with freedom itself we have become uncertain of the limits of the human. We do not know how to discover what the range and the quality of the capacities and experiences are that are to be denominated human, and unique to humanity, we do not know how to discover what is to be denominated non-human. We do not know what it is in our power to know. Yet paradoxically, it is these uncertainties, or, rather, the acknowledgment of them, that becomes the feature most clearly aligning those currently professing humane studies with humanists of the past. After the commitment to the intrinsic importance of the subject comes the indeflectible obligation to examine critically every affirmation, every disposition, the minds of conscious individuals entertain. This insistence on criticism, such questioning of authority as Erasmus represented so persuasively, differs from Pyrrhonism and from the usual manifestations of the Cartesian spirit in being founded on ideas of inherent worth, in the matter before it and in the undertaking. The classical humanist clings to essential doubt even as he holds fast to belief in worth.

And thus with what is being offered us currently with so much sophistication and passion. School upon school presents us highly articulated schemes in which the appeal is made to one or another of the senses attached to humanism. The very thoroughness of the arguments leads us to call upon the scepticism natural to the unconverted, to say nothing of the uninstructed. To be particular: Marxists forward the position that man is the product of historic forces, and when these reach their fulfillment a new man will have come into existence, freed from egoism, untrammeled in the triumph of collectivity. This goes by the name of "Marxian humanism." For the atheist existentialist it is his liberty alone that distinguishes each human from the absurd universe, and the hope for each of us lies in asserting absolute freedom. Sartre finds the term humanism acceptable here. For the positivist man is in all respects, his consciousness included, part and parcel of the material universe, and in acknowledging this he obtains such freedom from illusion as will enable him to control circumstance. For the Freudian human nature is distinguished by forces of which he is ignorant, that govern him through their innate energy by contrivance and subterfuge, and his fulfillment depends upon his ability to cope with them. For the rationalist man is a spirit sufficient unto himself, a free conscience in perpetual progress.

All these are "humanisms" but they are allied to philosophies that aim to provide explanations of the place of humans in all else, and consequently are absorbed in comprehensive philosophical systems. The layman, however, whenever provided with the elaborate super-structures in a scheme of thought feels justified in maintaining his reserve — he has seen too much come and go, and there are those learned enough to remind him that although it was once said, "So Newton came, and all was light," so Newton, too, came into the shadows. Henri Foçillon made the point in writing of the Middle Ages, the humanism of the learned depends on the humanism of the unlearned.

The bed-rock belief of the humanist is that no one may take anything on compulsion. With respect to doctrine each must cope with what is offered him not in mere obstinacy but in the light of such understanding as he has gained from experience and from what he owes to tradition. He may be unlearned but he possesses capacities that when decently equipped enable him to hold Marx and Freud and the latest determinists up to the light, to require they satisfy his questions. He may be baffled by the terminology of the phenomenologists as by that of the macro-economists or psychoanalysts, but he has for touchstone not only his mother-wit, he has learned the prudent management of abstractions and he has a high regard for coherence. He has learned to think and to express himself in ways the cultivation of rationality in the ancient world has passed on to him. He is, one way or another, civilized in the western manner. He may not be skilled in philosophy, but however far or however little he pursues his questions, and however pertinacious in demanding resolution, he will be giving witness to Whitehead's remark that all subsequent thought is a footnote to the philosophy of Plato and Aristotle. As for the student or scholar, he need not be deep in their works — he need only know why and how they set about what they did. It will not take much to show him how theirs has always been his own way, that he is in pretty much the same position as the gentleman who learned he had always been speaking prose.

II

In soliciting and attaining relationships with others and indeed with all that the senses and the arts present to us we are as intent upon what we make of them for the future as for the present. We approach all that is momentary with a desire to retain what we judge confirms us in our capacity to become wiser and better. Each satisfaction and enjoyment we take as preparing for further accretions, and to be endowing us with the power to confer these same joys on others. So that memory becomes the guarantor of creation, the instant of communication fruitful, and the clearest of faiths justified.

Although most myserious in its ways our nature winnows and selects and directs what we are holding to as of such worth —

Dear God, and all that mighty heart is lying still!

The remembrance of the sight of London in the early morning not only lights up the future, what we shall learn to cherish more and more as time passes of the beauty in the life of a great city, it helps settle more and more firmly the lines and the complexes of the growth of our natures and our spirits and our thinking, it helps make certain that the man of whom the child is the father is ever true to what that child promised.

The words renewing the rembrance add another wealth, chiefly a more vivid setting for the cherished sight in fixing its place in time, its particular worth in the light of all else we cherish, and still hold to. It is not only that the lovely and the powerful and the awful in the right expression grace our remembrance, they extend our thought.

Hamlet's words to Horatio tell of such trust as all require —

> blest are those
> Whose blood and judgment are so well commeddled
> That they are not a pipe for Fortune's finger
> To sound what stop she please. Give me that man
> That is not passion's slave, and I will wear him
> In my heart's core, ay, in my heart of heart,
> As I do thee.

There is hardly a day in which this notion is not before us, there have been times we have proven it, but whenever these particular words come to mind we see this truth in the light of what we are making of the passing of time. Heard the first time the words help us define our trust, thereafter they confirm our dedication.

What is it we retain? And what determines the selections and emphases? A child remembers sounds and in time meanings to go with them. Much is offered him, much is excluded. Much is determined by the particular vessel he is, some senses sharper than others; much is fixed in the pattern of his growth through the particular environment and language he is offered. And so the adult limits or extends these confines, and as the problems become more complex, the choices more and more restrained, the factor of divine necessity — Leonardo's phrase for the ultimate freedom — is more and more his, the end more and more within his power. Michelangelo in old age has more choices and more urgent choices before him than Michelangelo the youth. The Rondanini Pietà more complexly responds to the wealth of his experience than the Santo Spirito Crucifix to his innocence. But the latest work even then does not exhaust the promise of the first, so rich is this vessel of the human spirit, this child, this beginning.

And then, as circumstances call for deeds — requiring judgment, courage, foresight; depending, it may be, on what Milton's Samson called "dim rousings" — he finds in the light these images and stories offer what deserves his approbation. Above all else they confirm his valuing of trust and faithfulness.

So that these infinite choices over the years for which "he cannot," in Bergson's words, "give the reason, nevertheless have their reason," and the right actions are what enable the child to grow into the man that is true to the child, that best accommodate his amibitions and energies and passions and inclinations, to take such a form in character that in his maturity he is able to square his thought with his nature, because his thought has revealed to him through the choices he has made that the laws governing life are the laws of nature, and thought that discovers the relations of love and aspiration to his life with others is revealing the power that in his forming has determined his end, the harmonizings of his energies, the direction of his existence, the substantiation of his faiths. In the neglect of which it would be said of Faustus —

Cut is the branch that might have grown full straight.

Time passes irrevocably, and the young person understands this quickly, and so gives himself unstintedly and absolutely, recklessly, to what attracts him. By nature and disposition more than morally he gives himself as to commitment, and in the giving, in time, he discovers that there must also be commitment, and in making choices, keeping faith, honoring principle, he possesses what alone enriches his givings enough to insure their contribution to his ends as a man.

So much will come about as it were magically — a stray word picked up from a girl or a book, a particular beauty, a brilliant play in a game — these and countless other unforeseeable consonances, day after day, passing in unpremeditated wonder, or sloth or work, come in time to seem to him the stuff of his interest, the form of his purposes, the malleable stuff of time his nature and chance and some purposeful power he can only identify as what occasioned his being are making into what he comes to know he must become. In that delight he finds in being and becoming, in the response to these marvellous intimations, in the very idea of a prospect, a future, he has learned that in exercising the power of choice he is contributing to nature what it needs, the invigoration of commitment.

And so the humanities, with their limited use for objectivity, illustrating so many right choices — aesthetically the right balance and proportion, intellectually and morally the faithful representation of the way things are — teach him what science also can but less movingly, that a hair's line separates success and failure, that everything can ride on a single throw, that temporizing is out. In short, he is right to take things seriously, responsibly committed — and so he continues to ring true, knowing that perspective depends on this. The absolute conviction of the reality of freedom and the unquestioning assumption of responsibility for the consequences of his acts are continually renewed through the expressions that bind him as nothing else does to the race.

Index

Peristiany, Jean G., 88 n. 2
Petrarch, 21, 22, 24, 25, 53, 104
Phaedrus, 57
Piaget, Jean, 9, 10 n. 8, 17
Pico della Mirandola, 9
Pindar, 52, 54, 60
Plato, 15, 46, 48, 53, 56, 58, 65, 70 n. 21, 97, 104, 114
Plot, Robert, 102
Plotinus, 58, 104
Polanyi, Michael, 15, 25, 71 n. 26, 95
Polyeucte, 35
Pope, Alexander, 78
Popper, Karl, 34, 92
Positivism, 13-16, 18, 30-1, 78, 84, 86-7, 88, 91, 95, 110, 113
Pragmatism, 85, 86
Prayer Book, 93
Pre-Raphaelites, 17
Prince, The, 100, 102-103
Prometheus, 19, 53, 67, 112
Prospero, 6, 45
Protagoras, 50, 51

Racine, 17, 36
Robert, Fernand, 10 n. 9, 70 n. 18
Rorsach tests, 28, 112
Roubouczek, Paul, 70 n. 14
Ryle, Gilbert, 108

Sartre, J.-P., 26, 51, 113
Satan, 68
Schlipp, P. A., 98 n. 1 (Henryk Skolimowsky)
Shakespeare, 15, 17, 38, 43, 44, 45, 54, 60, 62, 109
Shoemaker, Sidney, 70 n. 15

Sidney, Philip, 24, 58
Simey, T. S., 10 n. 2
Snell, Bruno, 8
Socrates, 20, 22, 54-7, 60, 62, 72 n. 32, 73 n. 32, 78, 93, 103
Sophocles, 39
Sperry, Roger W., 70 n. 13
Spiegelberg, Samuel, 71 n. 23
Spock, Benjamin, 35
Strauss, Leo, 10 n. 1
Stravinsky, Igor, 32
Swift, Jonathan, 12

Tacitus, 109
Tammelo, Ilmar, 66, 73 n. 33
Telemachus, 41
Teleology, 69 n. 7
Terence, 76, 77
Thales, 15
Theataetus, 50
Timaeus, 65
Tintoretto, 44
Toffanin, Giuseppe, 2
Trojan Women, The, 108
Twain, Mark, 22

Ulysses, 47, 49, 53
UNESCO, 86

Valéry, Paul, 52, 72 n. 32
Vivas, Eliseo, 82
Vives, Ludovico, 24
Voltaire, François-Marie, 95

Weber, Max, 3, 4, 100
Whitehead, Alfred North, 114
Wittgenstein, Ludwig, 26
Wordsworth, William, 115